RESEARCH AND DEVELOPMENT IN INDIAN INDUSTRY

ABOUT THE AUTHOR

DR. G.C. BERI (*b.* 1932) obtained his B.Com. and M.Com. degrees, both First Ciass, from the Agra University in 1951 and 1953 respectively. Subsequently, he studied at the London School of Economics & Political Science and wrote the thesis on "Measurements of Production and Productivity in Indian Industry with Special Reference to Some Methodological Aspects". For this thesis, submitted to the University of London, Dr. Beri was awarded the degree of Ph.D. and also the Bowley Prize of the London School of Economics.

In 1974-75, Dr. Beri was awarded a Senior Visiting Fellowship tenable at the Queen Elizabeth House, Oxford, for one academic year.

Dr. Beri was a member on the panel of Commerce of the University Grants Commission for a period of two years. He has worked in several organisations, including the National Council of Applied Economic Research, New Delhi. Prior to his retirement in June 1992, he was Professor, Head and Dean, Faculty of Management Studies, M.S. University of Baroda.

Dr. Beri has a number of published papers to his credit. He has been listed in some international WHO's WHO and Directories published both from the U.S.A. and the U.K.

RESEARCH AND DEVELOPMENT IN INDIAN INDUSTRY

G.C. BERI
Former Professor and Dean
Faculty of Management Studies
M.S. University of Baroda

CONCEPT PUBLISHING COMPANY, NEW DELHI 110059

ISBN 81-7022-481-0

First Published 1993

Published and Printed by
Ashok Kumar Mittal
Concept Publishing Company
A/15-16, Commercial Block, Mohan Garden
NEW DELHI 110059 (India)

Lasertypeset by
Printing Express,
H-13, Bali Nagar,
NEW DELHI 110015

PREFACE

Research and Development (R&D) is a subject of considerable importance. Advanced countries of the world have given greater attention to Research and Development which is reflected in technological advance that they have made from time to time in different spheres. This is one of the factors that has contributed to their economic development. In India, like many other developing countries, Research and Development has not received adequate attention so far. All the same, there is now increasing realisation that something ought to be done to promote it.

This book is the result of a project study undertaken by me at the M.S. University of Baroda. The University Grants Commission provided financial assistance that enabled me to take up the study. Subsequently, it also granted me publishing subsidy which made it possible to publish it. I am extremely grateful to the University Grants Commission for both these financial grants.

Initially, the study was envisaged to be comprehensive as it intended to undertake a detailed survey of R&D units for collecting primary data. However, on account of certain difficulties (including the meagre payment to Research Assistants) over which I had no control, it became necessary to change the approach. It was decided to use a mail questionnaire to collect the required data from R & D units. Unfortunately, the response to this mail questionnaire was extremely poor mainly on account of the hesitation on the part of industrial units to part with any information pertaining to their R&D projects. Some of them refused to give the data sought on the plea that such data had already been given to the Department of Science & Technology (DST). As the DST would not provide access to individual questionnaires, the study made use of the published statistics of the DST. Had the data from individual R&D units been available, certain hypotheses could have been statistically tested and the study would have been quite comprehensive. However, it has been possible to undertake a short survey to elicit the opinion of R&D managers. This has enabled me to know the problems faced by them in carrying out their day-to-day R&D projects and their suggestions to promote R&D activity. I am grateful to all the R&D managers who have furnished the information sought in the opinion survey.

This study was completed in December 1991. At that time the latest statistics on Research and Development related to 1988-89. The Department of Science and Technology brings out these statistics every two years. When the study was under print, the DST's new publication came out bringing the statistics on R&D upto 1990-91. In view of this, I thought it proper to update the study especially its Chapter 3 on "Major Trends in R&D Activity in India" incorporating the latest statistics. I am extremely thankful to my publishers, the Concept Publishing Company, for allowing me to do so.

While I am conscious of certain limitations of the study, I think that even in its present modest form, it has reached certain findings that have become all the more relevant at the present juncture when the Indian economy is undergoing the process of liberalisation. It is earnestly hoped that the findings of the study as well as the suggestions made herein will receive due attention of the government, industry and technical and research institutions, so that R&D activity can be geared up in India significantly and this, in turn, would make the Indian economy more progressive and more competitive than hitherto.

G.C. BERI

CONTENTS

LIST OF TABLES

1

INTRODUCTION

Research and Development (R&D) is a subject of growing importance all over the world. This is because of a number of factors. First, one finds that R&D activity is related to economic development. Many rich countries of today are those where R&D activity has been accorded an important place and *vice versa*. There are, however, instances where expenditure on R&D is high and yet the growth rate of the economy is low. This suggests that there are other factors necessary for the growth which are lacking there. We would accept the premise that there is a positive relationship between R&D activity and economic growth. There is a good deal of evidence to support this. Second, in the case of depleting natural resources such as coal and other minerals, properly directed R&D activity would help in providing substitutes. Finally, developing countries such as India are striving to expand their export trade which could only be possible if they are not behind their competitors in technical knowledge. All these factors signify the importance of R&D activity.

However, R&D has received only scant attention so far from researchers as is borne out by a few studies made on the subject. In order to overcome this deficiency, it is necessary that a series of studies covering various aspects of R&D be made. Such studies should identify the problem areas, suggest corrective measures and finally lead to the evolution of meaningful policy on R&D with a long-term perspective. The proposed study is an effort in this direction.

Before we indicate the scope and methodology of the present study, it seems worthwhile to know the concepts of research and development.

Concepts of Research and Development

The term 'research' signifies the process which leads to the advancement of knowledge. According to the National Science

Foundation of the United States,[1] scientific research is systematic and intensive study directed towards fuller scientific knowledge of the subject studied. It could be of two types, namely, basic or pure research and applied research. Basic research is experimental or theoretical work undertaken primarily to acquire new knowledge of the underlying foundation of phenomena and observable facts without any particular application or use in view.[2] As Keith Norris and John Vaizey point out, the former is undertaken with no specific commercial objective, while the latter tackles problems with immediate commercial potential.[3] Though one may be able to distinguish basic research from applied research, the distinction between the two at times gets blurred. Several firms may be engaged in basic research which does not have any immediate commercial use. However, it may be commercially potential as otherwise firms would not undertake it at all.

The National Science Foundation defines 'development' as "the systematic use of the scientific knowledge directed towards production of useful materials, devices, systems or methods, including design and development of prototypes and processes."[4] It is the process of selecting the most promising research results and using them to create new products or processes. A comparison of the definitions of 'research' and 'development' as given by the National Science Foundation shows that the latter lays emphasis on the application of scientific knowledge. Since all processes or products are not likely to be profitable in given market conditions, development involves the identification of commercially most promising processes or products and discarding others. It will be seen that commercial objectives become overwhelmingly important in the development stage of a new product. An integral part of development activity is design which involves a comprehensive examination of commercial and production possibilities. Finally, when a new production process is introduced or a production line is set up to produce a new product, one may regard it as the final outcome of development. In this context, one may also like to know the meaning of a related term 'innovation' which takes place towards the end of development phase. Innovation is the embodiment of new knowledge into actual productive processes. However, there are certain improvements which take place subsequently. This is because certain limitations or deficiencies become apparent only when production takes place on a fairly large scale. In other words, some development takes place subsequently to innovation which goes on to signify that there is overlapping of research, development and production.[5]

Research and Development – A Recent Phenomenon in India

In 1973, the Department of Science and Technology (DST), Government of India introduced a scheme under which R&D units apply to the department for registration. This scheme is presently being handled by the Department of Scientific and Industrial Research. The DST carries out a questionnaire survey on various aspects of R&D among R&D units. On the basis of the responses received, Table 1.1 gives the break-up of R&D units according to the plan period in which they were set up.

TABLE 1.1: Setting up of R&D Units According to Plan Period

	Plan Period	No. of units set up
1.	Prior to First Plan (upto 1950)	27
2.	First Five Year Plan (1951-52 to 1955-56)	12
3.	Second Five Year Plan (1956-57 to 1960-61)	23
4.	Third Five Year Plan (1961-62 to 1965-66)	55
5.	Annual Plans (1966-67 to 1968-69)	45
6.	Fourth Five Year Plan (1969-70 to 1973-74)	170
7.	Fifth Five Year Plan (1974-75 to 1978-79)	238
8.	Annual Plan (1979-80)	58
9.	Sixth Five Year Plan (1980-81 to 1984-85)	290
10.	Seventh Five Year Plan (1985-86 to 1989-90)	296

The figures given in Table 1.1 clearly indicate that research and development in Indian industry was very meagre upto 1950 as there were only 27 units that had facilities for R&D. Since 1969-70 the number of new R&D units has increased in each subsequent Five Year Plan period. One finds that on an average 50 new R&D units were set up each year during the period 1969-70 to 1989-90 in contrast to only 8 units during the preceding plan period. This shows that R&D activity in Indian industry is of relatively recent origin.

Scope and Methodology of the Study

The present study is concerned with research and development carried out by industrial firms, in the public and private sectors, in

India. It is based both on primary and secondary data. The primary data relate to the opinion survey of R&D managers conducted by the researcher. In addition, information collected by interviewing senior executives in selected enterprises has been used to have a better understanding of problems faced in respect of R&D activity in a wider perspective.

As regards secondary data, mostly the data published by the Department of Science and Technology, Government of India have been used. These statistics are most authentic so far as R&D activity is concerned. It may be added that the study as was envisaged earlier was also to be based on the primary data to be collected through a mail questionnaire from industrial firms registered with the Department of Science and Technology. A questionnaire was designed for this purpose and it was sent out to a number of industrial enterprises. However, as there was an extremely poor response from them, it was decided to use intensively whatever R&D statistics were already available.

Contents of the Study

The study contains in all nine chapters. The first chapter deals with some conceptual aspects and describes the main approach adopted by the researcher. It also highlights that R&D is a relatively recent phenomenon in India.

Chapter 2 first deals with the concept and the process of technological change. This is followed by a discussion on the relationship between technological change and the economic performance at the firm's level.

Chapter 3 deals with major trends in R&D activity in India. The analysis is based on the official statistics on R&D brought out by the Department of Science and Technology, Government of India. It gives a comprehensive analysis, covering such aspects as R&D expenditure by sectors, R&D expenditure by major scientific agencies, R&D expenditure in selected industries, R&D intensity in public and private sectors, international comparisons of R&D expenditure, growth of patents in India, R&D output by sectors in India.

Chapter 4 focuses on R&D at the micro level. It describes R&D practices in selected enterprises belonging to different industry groups. At the end, an approach to generalisation has been made by identifying some major factors that have contributed to the successful

R&D in selected enterprises.

Chapter 5 analyses opinion survey data. The analysis is based on the information collected through a mail survey of R&D managers. The objective of this survey was to know at first hand what R&D managers feel about R&D activity in their enterprises. The main hurdles faced by R&D managers have been brought out. In addition, some useful suggestions made by them for strengthening R&D activity are specified.

Chapter 6 deals with institutional collaborations in R&D activity. It discusses collaboration between IITs and industry in some detail, highlighting some of the recommendations of the Review Committee, especially relating to the setting up of the Industrial Foundation, development of entrepreneurship, industry-research-education nexus. This is followed by a discussion on collaboration between university and industry, pointing out barriers to university-industry interaction. Towards the end, the chapter gives a detailed account of the National Research Development Corporation (NRDC) reviewing its performance from 1983-92. It makes certain suggestions so that the NRDC can play a more effective role than hitherto in promoting R&D in India.

Chapter 7 is devoted to the government policy relating to R&D. It first emphasizes the need for having a fresh look on incentives so that they can be made more useful. The discussion goes far beyond this and pertains to broader issues regarding country's technology policy. In this context, the chapter emphasizes the need for strengthening technology information and development of human resources. Towards the end, it briefly covers the patterns of government intervention in different countries. It finally concludes by citing the example of Japan, emphasizing the need for integrating industrial and technological policies.

Chapter 8 focuses on R&D statistics in India. It first gives a brief account of the evolution of R&D statistics in the country. This is followed by a detailed and critical appraisal of R&D statistics. Major limitations of R&D statistics especially in regard to R&D expenditure are pointed out. In addition, it makes a number of suggestions for improving and enlarging the scope of such statistics. Some of the suggestions are extremely relevant and they will considerably improve the quality of R&D statistics, if implemented.

Finally, Chapter 9 brings out the major conclusions emerging from this study. Some of the conclusions are in the form of specific suggestions covering a wide area. Since these suggestions are based on a comprehensive and objective analysis of the most recent data coupled with discussions with senior R&D personnel, they seem to be extremely relevant. The suggestions, if carried out, will not only strengthen R&D activity in India in terms of the expenditure involved but will also give it a meaningful direction. As the country is on the threshold of a technological revolution, it is imperative at this juncture that it must gear-up its indigenous R&D by adopting suitable measures.

NOTES

1. National Science Foundation: *Methodological Aspects of Statistics on Research and Development, Costs and Manpower*, Washington, 1959, p.74.
2. Stoneman, Paul: *The Economic Analysis of Technology Policy*, Oxford, Clarendon Press, 1987, p.13
3. Keith Norris and John Vaizey : *The Economics of Research and Technology*, London, George Allen & Unwin Ltd., 1973, p.21.
4. National Science Foundation : *Op. cit.*
5. Keith Norris and John Vaizey : *Op. cit.*, p.21.

2

TECHNOLOGICAL CHANGE

Introduction

This chapter first deals with the concept and the process of technological change. This is followed by a discussion on the relationship between technological change and the economic performance at the firm's level. The discussion is essentially based on studies done in some advanced countries. At the end, the chapter brings out that technological change is quite rewarding to countries in their export trade as well.

Concept of Technological Change

Let us first start with the concept of technological change. According to Schumpeter[1] technological change covers five main types of technological dynamism in an economy. These are: (1) new processes, by which is meant new ways of using existing resources to produce existing products; (2) new products, encompassing the use of existing processes and materials to produce completely new or changed versions of existing goods and services; (3) new sources or types of raw materials, covering discoveries of new sources of supply or changes in the raw materials available; (4) new markets, either in a geographic sense or in the sense of applications of existing products to new uses; and (5) new organisational methods, that is new means of controlling and organising productive inputs. This shows technological change can take several forms.

Stages in Technological Change[2]

There are three stages in the technological change: invention, innovation and diffusion. The first stage is invention which relates to the generation of new ideas. It is marked by discovery or a state of new existence, usually at the lab or bench. The second stage is innovation which involves the development of new ideas so that they can be exploited on a commercial basis. Thus, when an invention is transformed in the form of a new product or a new process, it is known as innovation. As Edward B. Roberts has put it:

Innovation = Invention + Exploitation

The third stage is diffusion, which indicates that different firms have adopted the particular innovation in the form of a new product or a new process. By its very nature, diffusion is a time-consuming process. It may also be noted that not all inventions will lead to innovation and, likewise, not all innovations such as a new product or process will be successfully diffused.

There are certain features of this process of technological change. First, it is time-intensive. A good deal of time is needed from invention to innovation to diffusion. On the basis of past experience in the Western economies, it is found that approximately a period of thirteen years elapses when an invention is transformed in the form of a new product or process and then any time up to fifty years is needed for the diffusion of the new product or process across the firms. This is shown in Fig. 2.1.

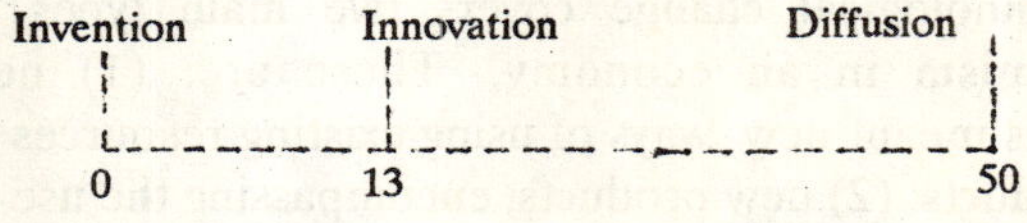

FIG. 2.1: Time in years

Second, the technological change is a continuous process. This means that even when earlier innovations are getting diffused in an economy, new innovations as also new inventions are taking place in that economy.

Third, the technological change is not a self-contained process though it may seem to be so at first sight. This means that technological advances are not isolated from one another and there may be both international and cross-process linkages between one technological advance and others. Whatever technological advances are taking place in the present will be dependent upon past advances in knowledge and technology. Similarly, they will have certain repercussions for technology into the future.

Finally, as no economy can operate in isolation, there is an international dimension of technological change. A country need not produce all the technologies needed. It may import latest technology from abroad in certain spheres and develop its own technology in other spheres.

Marketing as a Major Source of Innovation

What are the major sources of innovation? Although there are several factors but they can be classified into two groups, namely, technology push and demand pull situations. Several authors have tried to ascertain whether an innovation especially in the form of a new product has resulted on account of technological developments or prospective demand considerations. In this connection, it may be noted that Didier C.L. Bonnet[3] asserts that the degree of integration between R&D and marketing is strongly correlated with the extent of industrial product success. Many studies have consistently reported that a strong link between R&D and marketing was one of the important factors for the success of new product development. Despite this, there is a dilemma about this. Some people are concerned whether a new product idea has resulted from a technology push situation or a market-pull situation. Utterback provided a summary of several studies on this aspect (Table 2.1).

TABLE 2.1: **Source of Innovation**

Study	Proportion of innovation from market, mission or production needs (%)	Proportion from technical opportunities (%)
Baker *et al*	77	23
Carter and Williams	73	27
Goldhar	69	31
Sherwin and Isenson	66	34
Langrish *et al*	66	34
Myers and Marquis	78	22
Tannenbaum *et al*	90	10
Utterback	75	25

Source : Bonnet, Didier C.L. : "Nature of the R&D/ Marketing Cooperation in the Design of Technologically Advanced New Industrial Products", *R&D Management*, Vol.16, No.2, 1986, p.120.

From the figures given in Table 2.1, it is evident that the market pull rather than technology-push stimulus was far more important in successful technological innovations. Broadly, three out of every four successful innovations are stimulated from need recognition, while the remainder are initiated from the availability of technical opportunities. In other words, demand-pull rather than technology-push is the more important factor contributing to technological innovations. This indicates that recognition of a genuine need is the most important factor in starting an innovation. Often marketing aspect is taken for granted and this results into avoidable losses on account of new product failures.

Jervis[4] has done a study to ascertain the characteristics of successful innovations. The study concerned itself with 70 innovations equally divided between successes and failures. These innovations related to two industries, chemicals, and scientific instruments. The study found that successful innovations were superior in the following areas: (1) innovation-inclined management, (2) understanding user needs, (3) marketing and sales performance, (4) efficiency of development, and (5) effectiveness of communications. It will be seen that two of these characteristics namely Nos. (2) and (3) indicate the importance of marketing in making an innovation successful. In fact, an important barrier to technological innovation pertains to marketing. In particular, inadequacy and uncertainty of market information, difficulties in expanding the existing markets as well as in identifying new markets are considered the main impediments.

Technological Change and Economic Performance[5]

At this stage, we may ask a pertinent question : what is the role of technological change in economic performance? We would confine the discussion to only two aspects of the performance of an economy. The first is productivity growth and rates of return. The second is success of the economy in the sphere of international trade.

The subject of relationship between technological change and economic performance has attracted the attention of several economists from time to time. However, modern work on this subject was initiated by three almost contemporaneous studies of the U.S. economy. These studies were done by Fabricant,[6] Abromovitz[7] and Solow,[8] the last-named having been the most influential.

Solow studied the non-farm American economy over the period 1909-49 and concluded that the output of the non-farm sector was related to the inputs of labour and capital, and time according to a Cobb-Douglas production function with constant returns to scale.

Solow estimated that had there been no change in capital and labour, the non-farm American economy could have growth at the rate of 1.5 per cent per annum. Based on this finding Solow concluded that as much as nine per cent increase in productivity (output per man) could be attributed to the residual or time factor and only about 10 per cent to increases in capital per man.

Since the residual has frequently been taken as technological change, Solow's study was interpreted as nine per cent of the increase in U.S. labour productivity was due to technological change. The question that arose was : Could the residual be taken as equivalent to technological change? Some economists addressed themselves to this problem. Denison,[9] for example, tried to give a break-up of this residual into its constituent parts. He concluded that about 40 per cent of the total increase in national income per head could be attributed to 'advances in knowledge' namely technological change.

Subsequent studies moved further from the residual analysis and considered technological change as a separate input into the production process. Though it was still felt that changes in production would take place as time advances, the main focus was on research and development as an important input into the production process. It was argued that any expenditure on research and development would add to the existing stock of knowledge. Thus, contributions to the stock of knowledge along with capital and labour would generate output in the economy.

It may be pointed out at this stage that estimates based on R&D expenditure do not necessarily reflect the importance of technological change in its entirety. This is because R&D activity is not the only source of new technology. For example, a firm may buy new machines embodying new technology and by using such machines may attain higher productivity. Now, this new technology would not be reflected in that firm's R&D expenditure.

Another criticism of the production function approach, as used in these studies, is that it is relevant in the context of output of a given mix. When the output involves a changing mix of products, the production function approach is not suitable. This is because the measurement of production involves aggregation over different products and the aggregation is unable to reflect the changes in the product-mix.

Another comment on R&D expenditure as a source of technological change is that R&D expenditure can have an impact only when diffusion takes place. As we have noticed in the beginning of this chapter, the process of technological change involves invention, innovation and diffusion, which is a long-drawn process. R&D is largely confined to the first two stages of technological process. Now, the impact of diffusion of new technology would obviously be far greater on productivity than R&D expenditure confined to the first two stages. This implies that one ought to consider the cost involved in diffusion while ascertaining the contribution of technological change on productivity. In case diffusion costs are ignored, as it normally happens, returns on R&D are obviously over-estimated.

A Conflicting Study

Sherman Gee[10] takes the position that R&D and productivity are not positively correlated. He thinks that a positive relationship between the two may be entirely illusory. He goes on to observe : "Funding for R&D is a measure only of the effort to broaden the science-technology base. However, the relationship between the science-technology base and productivity improvement is not a close one. The path from R&D investment to productive output is typically a long and arduous one, lasting many years. Hence there is no assurance that the technical knowledge base resulting from R&D will be effectively applied towards greater economic output – new and better products and processes." Continuing with this line of argument, Sherman Gee gives an example of a study on the relationship between industrial R&D and productivity growth in the selected manufacturing industries (chemicals, metals, electrical and non-electrical machinery, and instruments) in the 12 industrial nations of the OECD for the period 1963-1973. The analysis revealed that there was no clear correlation between industrial R&D intensity and productivity. However, it may be noted that there is an overwhelming evidence available from several other studies which indicate a close positive relationship between industrial R&D and productivity. In case of the absence of such a relationship, there must have been some other factors that had offset the productivity growth.

Sherman Gee goes on a step further and gives an example of Nobel prize awardees. Taking the number of Nobel prizes awarded per unit of population as a measure of the basic research output of a country, he found that there was an inverse relationship between basic research output and productivity. Countries with a large number of Nobel prize laurates over the period 1961-76 were, in descending order, the U.K., the U.S.A., West Germany, and Japan. However, the ranking of nations on the basis of productivity growth during the same period was almost exactly the opposite : Japan, West Germany, the U.K. and the U.S.A.

It may be emphasized that basic research output and productivity need not be positively correlated. Nobel prizes relate to outstanding discoveries/inventions achieved by an individual or a group of individuals. As such it is too much to expect that such discoveries/inventions would soon have impact on productivity over the entire economy. The diffusion process based on a Nobel prize, would be spread over a very long period. It should therefore, be clear that this example of relating the number of Nobel prizes awarded per unit of population with the productivity in industrial countries is inappropriate and misplaced. We would reiterate that it is reasonable to assume that technological innovation intensity is positively related to productivity. A number of studies done in advanced industrial countries support this assumption.

The foregoing comments were in respect of the relationship between the number of Nobel prizes per unit of population and productivity. However, one would expect a close relationship between the number of patents granted and industrial productivity. This is because a patent shows the development of a new product/process which is expected to yield special benefit to the concerned party for a specified period. Even here, diffusion of a new technology across several units would lead to higher productivity, though it would take considerable time. This highlights the importance of diffusion of technology in raising industrial productivity.

Estimates of Rates of Return to Investment in R&D

A number of studies of returns to industrial R&D have been made in developed countries. These studies show varying rates of return on R&D investment realised by firms, at least as high as that realised on alternative investments. Mansfield *et al.*[11] report on 17 case studies of innovation for which the median private rate of return was 25 per cent. Griliches[12] finds that returns to R&D for large industrial firms in the United States vary from 30 to 50 per cent.

Mairesse[13] and Sassenou reviewed statistical estimates of the impact of research on a firm's productivity. The review related to five economy-wide and four sector studies using cross-sectional, firm-level data. It covered seven U.S., five French and four Japanese studies. All these studies indicated positive R&D elasticities ranging from 14 to 42 per cent with a median of 27 per cent. Another set of firm-level studies carried out by Mairesse and Sassenou attempted to estimate rates of return directly. They concluded that for the three countries namely, U.S., France and Japan (during its imitation phase), private rates of return to R&D were at least as high as for other investments.

The above discussion relates to private rates of return. Social rates of return may be higher than private rates of return. This is because the individual firm is incapable of appropriability, or capturing completely the benefits from conducting R&D. According to a study conducted by Mansfield *et al*., the median social rate of return from major innovations was 56 per cent; the median private rate of return was 25 per cent.

What is the implication of a high rate of return to investment in R&D? As more of a factor of production is employed in production, the marginal factor productivity decreases. As such a high rate of return to investment in R&D implies that the country is not allocating its resources efficiently. It would be advisable for that country to transfer its resources used in activities that currently earn low rates of return to R&D activity where returns are higher. Thus, investment in R&D would increase up to that level when the marginal return to R&D is equivalent to "normal" return. In other words, high returns on R&D clearly show under-investment in R&D activity. This indicates that as technological changes are very important, an economy can derive substantial net gains from further investment in technology.

Technological Change and Export Performance

So far the discussion was confined to the impact of technological change on productivity. We now turn to another aspect viz. international trading performance. Stoneman[14] cites an example from an empirical study done by Soete in 1981. This study finds that a country's performance in the export trade is closely related to the degree of its innovativeness. The extent of innovativeness is judged by the number of successful patent applications by a country. The high degree of positive correlation between technological advance and export performance does indicate that success of a country in international trade depends on its technological superiority.

A pertinent issue here is that this technological superiority can be acquired not only by the innovations in the country itself but also by importing superior technology. In other words, a country need not undertake R&D on its own but import technology and yet put up a good performance in the sphere of international trade. This discussion only shows that improved technology (whether imported or indigenous) does have a positive effect on the export performance of a country. However, it is reasonable to assume that large scale import of technology may not be possible in a developing country on account of financial constraints and other relevant considerations.

Another point worth mentioning is that imported technology may be adapted to suit the requirements of the importing country. In such a case, the imported technology may lead to increase domestic R&D to a certain extent. For example, a study done by Deolalikar and Evenson[15] finds that industrial firms in India have responded to increased foreign invention by increasing their technology purchases from foreigners and increasing indigenous R&D.

Concluding Remarks

The discussion contained in this chapter has emphasized that technological change is a long-drawn process. A major source of technological change is the market potential say, of a new product. As regards technological change and economic performance, there appears to be close positive relationship between them. Although there are studies which question such a positive relationship, but a large number of other studies based on empirical data from different countries support the hypothesis that technological change and economic performance are positively correlated.

There is an ample evidence that a firm normally earns a high rate of return to investment in R&D. This shows that the country is not allocating its resources efficiently and it is advisable to transfer its resources to R&D where returns are relatively high. Further, the rates of return to R&D activity earned by an individual firm are private rates of return which are unable to capture the benefits accruing to the society. This means that the social rates of return are bound to be higher than the private rates of return. Finally, one finds that even in international trade, a country's performance in the export trade is closely related to the degree of its innovativeness.

NOTES

1. Schumpeter, J.A.: *Capitalism, Socialism and Democracy*, New York, Harper and Row, 1942.
2. Based on Stoneman, Paul: *The Economic Analysis of Technology Policy*, Oxford, Clarendon Press, 1987, pp. 8-12.
3. Bonnet, Didier C.L.: "Nature of the R&D/Marketing Cooperation in the Design of Technologically Advanced New Industrial Products", *R&D Management*, Vol.16, No.2, 1986.
4. Jervis, P.:"Innovation and Technology Transfer — The Roles and Characteristics of Individuals", *IEEE Transactions on Engineering Management*, EM- 22 (February 1975), pp. 19-27. Cited by Sherman Gee in publication mentioned in footnote 10.
5. This draws on Stoneman, Paul : *The Economic Analysis of Technology Policy*, Oxford, Clarendon Press, 1987, pp. 26-34.
6. Fabricant, S. : *Economic Progress and Economic Change*, Princeton, N.J., Princeton University Press, 1954.
7. Abromovitz, M. : "Resource and Output Trends in the United States since 1870", *American Economic Review* : Papers and Proceedings, 1956, Vol. 46, pp. 5-23.
8. Solow, R.M. : "Technological Change and the Aggregate Production Function", *Review of Economics and Statistics*, 1957, Vol. 39, pp. 312-20.
9. Denison, E.F. : *The Sources of Economic Growth in the United States*, New York, Committee for Economic Development, 1962.
10. Gee, Sherman : *Technology Transfer, Innovation, and International Competitiveness*, New York, John Willey & Sons, 1981, p.6.
11. Mansfield, E. *et al.* : *Technology Transfer, Productivity and Economic Policy*, New York, W.W. Norton, 1982.
12. Griliches, Z. : "Returns to Research and Development Expenditure in the Private Sector", *in* Kendrick, J.W. & B.N. Vaccare (eds.), *New Development in Productivity Measurement and Analysis*, Chicago, University of Chicago Press, 1980.
13. Cited by Evenson, Robert E. in his "Survey of Empirical Studies" included in the *World Bank Discussion Papers*, No. 112, 1990.
14. Stoneman, *Op. cit.*, p. 32.
15. Deolalikar, A.B. and R.E. Evenson : "Private Inventive Activity in Indian Manufacturing : Its Extent and Determinants", *in Science and Technology : Lessons for Development Policy* by R.E. Evenson and G. Rains, Boulder, Colo., Westview, 1990.

3

MAJOR TRENDS IN R&D ACTIVITY IN INDIA

Introduction

The purpose of this chapter is to highlight major aspects in the growth and pattern of R&D activity in India. The analysis is based on the official statistics brought out by the Department of Science and Technology (DST), Government of India. Although statistics published by the DST relate to such aspects as expenditure on R&D and related science and technology, R&D manpower, patents, etc., statistics of research and development expenditure are more comprehensive. Accordingly, R&D expenditure statistics are analysed in this chapter. Later in the chapter patent statistics too are analysed though in a limited way. At the end, the chapter sums up the main conclusions that emerge from this analysis.

Conceptual Aspects of R&D Expenditure Statistics

Before an analysis of R&D expenditure is attempted, a few related observations may be made here. First, R&D activity by itself is not important to economic growth unless it results in innovation which implies that outcome of R&D has been incorporated into production system. This may take one or more of the several forms such as production of an entirely new product, improvements in the existing product, improved production process, etc. In other words R&D expenditure is the initial aspect and much more needs to be done if it is to be really useful for practical purposes. It is now widely recognised that R&D must be followed by a continuous innovative chain linking scientific research, marketing research, invention, development design, tooling, first production and marketing of the new product.

It would be desirable to look into all these aspects and to analyse them so as to ascertain their contribution to economic growth. However, as some of these aspects are not quantifiable and as only scanty data are available on those which are amenable to measurement, analysis is generally confined to R&D expenditure statistics.

Further, in view of the fact as there exist many stages before R&D activity can be transformed into innovation, expenditure on R&D activity constitutes only a small proportion of the total cost of innovation. This would vary on account of the variations in the nature of R&D activity, its management, salary differentials of R&D personnel, etc.

According to a study, R&D expenditure constitutes merely 5 to 10 per cent of the total cost of successful product innovation. Despite the fact proportion of R&D expenditure is much smaller than the total cost of innovation, R&D expenditure series is readily available and, as such is used for analysis.

Another point that must be borne in mind is that there are certain conceptual difficulties in the measurement of R&D expenditure. For example, how does one allocate salary of staff engaged both in R&D and other routine activities? If industrial firms have exercised great care in such an allocation, then R&D expenditure statistics will be more reliable and *vice versa*. Furthermore, strict international comparisons of R&D expenditure may not be possible on account of wide salary differentials prevalent in different countries particularly as salaries of R&D personnel constitute a sizeable proportion of R&D expenditure.

A pertinent point that may be mentioned here is that there has been substantial increase in expenditure on defence and space research in some of the advanced countries. If expenditure on such research and development is included in the overall R&D expenditure, international comparisons get distorted especially when there are wide differences in defence R&D expenditure in different countries under comparison. In order to ensure comparability, it is desirable to use R&D expenditure series excluding expenditure on defence and space research. However, this may not always be possible on account of non-availability of expenditure on defence and space research, separately.

Another limitation in respect of international comparisons is that "monetary exchange rate does not always represent a true index of the comparative costs of conducting research in different countries". The problem is how to evolve a fully satisfactory measure of the comparative costs of conducting research in different countries. This is, no doubt, a formidable problem for statisticians. Though a few attempts have been made to measure the real cost of R&D in different countries, construction of an index of the comparative costs of R&D in different countries is not yet feasible.

The foregoing discussion points out conceptual and statistical limitations of R&D expenditure as an indicator of R&D activity. In view of these limitations, one has to exercise care in using this concept as also in interpreting the data. In the following paragraphs, an analysis of R&D expenditure in India is attempted to bring out its growth and pattern over the past several years.

Analysis of R&D Expenditure Statistics

During the period of 33 years, 1958-59 to 1991-92, R&D expenditure rose from a mere Rs. 23 crores to Rs. 4831 crores, the rise being more than 210 times (Table 3.1). The annual increase was much higher in the initial years on account of a very low base. If we omit these years, we find that increase in R&D expenditure varied from a low of 4.89 per cent in 1976-77 to a high of 29 per cent in 1984-85. In recent years, the annual increase has varied from 11.3 to 17.3 per cent over the preceding year.

TABLE 3.1: **Growth of R&D Expenditure**

Year	R&D Expenditure (Rs. in crores)	Percentage increase over the preceding year
1958-59	22.93	—
1965-66	68.39	—
1969-70	116.62	—
1974-75	291.60	—
1975-76	356.71	22.33
1976-77	374.16	4.89
1977-78	430.62	15.09
1978-79	528.60	22.75
1979-80	638.54	20.80
1980-81	760.52	19.10
1981-82	940.73	23.70
1982-83	1206.03	28.20
1983-84	1381.10	14.52
1984-85	1781.55	29.00
1985-86	2068.78	16.12
1986-87	2435.40	17.72
1987-88	2853.07	17.15
1988-89	3347.26	17.32
1989-90	3725.74	11.31
1990-91	4186.43	12.37
1991-92	4830.74	15.39

On the whole, one finds that there was a spectacular increase in R&D expenditure over this 33-year period. However, this impressive increase considerably fades away when one relates it to the Gross National Product (GNP). Relevant data in this regard are presented in Table 3.2.

TABLE 3.2: **R&D Expenditure in Relation to GNP**

Year	GNP (Rs. crores)	R&D Exp. (Rs. crores)	(3) as % of (2)
1974-75	63051	291.60	0.46
1975-76	66375	356.71	0.54
1976-77	71432	374.16	0.52
1977-78	80698	430.62	0.53
1978-79	87058	528.60	0.61
1979-80	95511	638.54	0.67
1980-81	122571	760.52	0.62
1981-82	142916	940.73	0.66
1982-83	158217	1206.03	0.76
1983-84	185047	1381.10	0.75
1984-85	206445	1781.55	0.86
1985-86	232730	2068.78	0.89
1986-87	258637	2495.87	0.96
1987-88	291789	2936.94	1.00
1988-89	346277	3471.81	1.00
1989-90	397396	3725.74	0.94
1990-91	468426	4186.43	0.89

In 1974-75, R&D expenditure was merely 0.46 per cent of GNP. It steadily rose over the 17 year period. It crossed one-half per cent mark in the following year and attained just one per cent of GNP in 1987-88. It remained at this level in 1988-89 as well. This percentage is extremely low as compared to the corresponding figures in many other countries, as will be seen later in this chapter.

Table 3.3 presents data on R&D expenditure by sector for selected years. It will be seen that the Central Government through its various departments had spent almost four-fifths of national R&D expenditure in 1991-92. The share of the State Governments was the lowest, being about eight per cent in 1991-92. Industrial units in the private sector accounted for 13 per cent of national R&D expenditure. This is not a happy picture as it reflects that private enterprises are still indifferent to R&D activity. This trend needs to be changed.

TABLE 3.3: **National R&D Expenditure by Sector**

(Rs. crores)

Year	Central Sector	State Sector	Private Sector	Total
1958-59	21.78	1.00	0.15	22.93
	(95.0)	(4.4)	(0.6)	(100.0)
1970-71	112.47	12.58	14.59	139.64
	(80.5)	(9.1)	(10.4)	(100.0)
1980-81	580.49	59.34	120.69	760.52
	(76.3)	(7.8)	(15.9)	(100.0)
1991-92	3827.33	371.94	631.47	4830.74
	(79.2)	(7.7)	(13.1)	(100.0)

Note: Figures in parentheses are percentages.

R&D expenditure by major scientific agencies in the Central Sector is shown in Table 3.4. From the figures it is clear that some new agencies namely. Department of Environment, Department of Ocean Development, Department of Non-Conventional Energy Sources and Department of Biotechnology have emerged in the eighties though R&D expenditure of all these agencies taken together is a little over one-tenth of the total R&D expenditure in the central sector. The Defence Research and Development Organisation which accounted for mere eight per cent of total R&D expenditure in 1958-59 showed an impressive increase of over 27 per cent in 1990-91. Further, out of 12 central agencies listed in the table, only five agencies accounted for as much as 77 per cent of total R&D expenditure by all central agencies. These are: Defence Research and Development Organisation, Department of Space, Department of Atomic Energy, Council of Scientific and Industrial Research and Indian Council of Agricultural Research. As the new agencies, mentioned earlier, are well-established and begin to intensify their R&D activity, the proportion of the top-five agencies in terms of R&D expenditure would come down in subsequent years.

Table 3.5 presents data on the allocation of R&D expenditure by major objectives. It is evident from these figures that almost one-fifth of R&D expenditure was in respect of defence. Allocation of R&D expenditure for promotion of agriculture and allied activities was 19.3 per cent followed by 16.5 per cent for the promotion of industrial development. These three objectives together accounted for 55 per cent of overall allocation of R&D expenditure. Then, of course, there were other objectives which were relatively less important than those just mentioned.

TABLE 3.4: R&D Expenditure by Major Scientific Agencies in the Central Sector

(Rs. crores)

Scientific Agencies	1958-59	%	1975-76	%	1980-81	%	1984-85	%	1990-91	%
Department of Atomic Energy	7.76	41.3	53.94	24.1	73.48	16.8	181.52	15.8	281.17	11.27
Council of Scientific & Indl. Research	5.10	27.1	37.11	16.6	69.00	15.7	126.36	11.0	250.00	10.03
Defence Research & Development Orgn.	1.50	8.0	52.17	23.3	79.70	18.2	37.32	29.3	685.00	27.48
Indian Council of Medical Research	0.51	2.7	3.32	1.5	9.00	2.0	26.06	2.3	43.70	1.75
Indian Council of Agri. Research	3.72	19.8	32.94	14.7	97.45	22.2	130.83	11.4	327.00	13.12
Department of Space	–	–	36.67	16.4	56.01	12.87	182.88	15.9	386.22	15.49
Department of Sci & Technolgy	0.22	1.1	5.25	2.3	40.64	9.3	96.16	8.4	181.14	7.37
Department of Electronics	–	–	2.38	1.1	5.41	1.2	4.11	0.3	24.16	0.97
Department of Ocean Environment	–	–	–	–	3.74	0.9	41.38	3.6	202.95	8.14
Department of Non-Conventional Energy Sources	–	–	–	–	4.00	0.9	10.69	0.9	32.26	1.29
Department of Bio-Technology	–	–	–	–	–	–	–	–	47.55	1.91
Department of Ocean Development	–	–	–	–	–	–	–	–	31.94	1.28
Total	18.81	100.0	223.78	100.0	438.43	100.0	1149.54	100.0	2493.09	100.00

TABLE 3.5: **Allocation of R&D Expenditure by Major Objectives, 1990-91**

(Rs. lakhs)

Objectives	Total	%age to total
Exploration and Assessment of Earth, Seas, Atmosphere	11477.43	2.75
Space	38820.99	9.30
Development of Agriculture, Forestry and Fishing	80620.43	19.31
Promotion of Industrial Development	68628.45	16.45
Production, Conservation and Distribution of Energy	19178.40	4.60
Development of Transport and Communication	23876.27	5.72
Development of Education Services	5145.39	1.23
Development of Health Services	18637.45	4.47
Social Development and other Socio-Economic Services	4481.66	1.07
Protection of Environment	18229.43	4.37
General Advancement of Knowledge	46398.71	11.11
Other items	1940.67	0.47
Defence	79851.79	19.14

So far the analysis was on the basis of total R&D expenditure i.e., industrial R&D and institutional R&D, the latter including Central and State governments. As our focus on this study is on research and development in the industrial sector, the analysis that follows is based on R&D expenditure in the industrial sector.

Table 3.6 presents data on industrial R&D expenditure for the period 1980-81 to 1990-91. It will be seen that expenditure on industrial R&D in relation to overall R&D expenditure is gradually declining although there was a rise in 1988-89 and 1989-90. It has come down from 27.2 per cent in 1980-81 to 23.2 per cent in 1990-91. This shows that non-industrial R&D expenditure which is incurred by Central and State governments rose steadily.

TABLE 3.6: **Industrial R&D Expenditure as a Percentage to Total**

Year	Industrial R&D Exp. (Rs.crores)	Total R&D Exp. (Rs.crores)	Percentage
1980-81	207.06	760.52	27.2
1981-82	254.55	940.73	27.1
1982-83	319.44	1206.03	26.5
1983-84	369.48	1381.10	26.8
1984-85	404.41	1781.55	22.7
1985-86	450.56	2068.78	21.8
1986-87	527.33	2435.40	21.7
1987-88	598.73	2853.07	21.0
1988-89	759.75	3347.26	22.7
1989-90	903.49	3725.74	24.2
1990-91	970.29	4186.43	23.2

Table 3.7 shows the break-up of industrial R&D expenditure by public and private sectors for the period 1980-81 to 1990-91. In view of increasing importance accorded to the public sector enterprises in the government's industrial policy, understandably public sector industrial R&D expenditure rose faster than that in the private sector. As a result, the former accounted for a larger percentage of the overall industrial R&D expenditure. In 1980-81, it was 41.7 per cent of total industrial R&D expenditure which rose to 45.8 per cent in 1990-91.

TABLE 3.7: **Industrial R&D Expenditure in Public and Private Sectors**

(Rs. crores)

Year	Public Sector	Private Sector	Total
1980-81	86.37	120.69	207.06
1981-82	107.55	147.00	254.55
1982-83	122.46	196.98	319.44
1983-84	161.65	207.83	369.48
1984-85	171.22	233.19	404.41
1985-86	198.62	251.94	450.56
1986-87	235.70	291.63	527.33
1987-88	288.46	310.27	598.73
1988-89	342.12	417.63	759.75
1989-90	412.90	490.59	903.49
1990-91	444.07	526.22	970.29

Table 3.8 shows the break-up of R&D units by the range of expenditure for the year 1990-91. The figures are given separately for the private and public sectors. It is evident from the table that an overwhelmingly large number of units in the private sector spend an extremely limited amount on R&D. In the private sector, out of 983 units as many as 396 units (40.3 per cent of the total number) spent up to Rs.10 lakhs on R&D. If we include next category, we find that 548 units (55.7 per cent of the total number) spent not more than Rs.20 lakhs on an average on their R&D activity. As regards the public sector units, 39 out of 155 units (25.2 per cent) spent up to Rs.10 lakhs on R&D while a little over one-third of the units spent upto Rs.20 lakhs. These percentages compare favourably with the corresponding figures for the private sector.

TABLE 3.8: Break-up of R&D Units by Range of R&D Expenditure

Range of R&D Expenditure (Rs. lakhs)	Private Sector		Public Sector	
	No. of Units	R&D Exp. (Rs. crores)	No. of Units	R&D Expenditure (Rs. crores)
0-10	396	18.63	39	1.68
10-20	152	22.30	16	2.41
20-30	97	23.88	9	2.38
30-50	118	46.52	16	6.21
50-100	107	77.19	22	15.73
100-200	61	84.05	18	27.52
200-300	15	37.15	9	22.94
300-400	15	51.74	4	14.55
400-500	8	36.68	5	22.01
500+	14	114.52	17	328.64
	983	512.66	155	444.07

Another interesting feature one finds is in respect of the highest category of R&D expenditure viz. Rs. 5 crores and more. There were 17 units in this category in the public sector which together accounted for an expenditure of about Rs.329 crores out of the total expenditure of Rs. 444 crores. This would amount to over 74 per cent of the aggregate expenditure in the public sector. In contrast, the corresponding figures for the private sector were merely 14 units out of 983 units accounting for about Rs.115 crores or 22.4 per cent of the aggregate expenditure. This highlights the wide gap between the large R&D units in the public sector and those in the private sector.

Table 3.9 presents data on R&D expenditure for selected industries for the two years 1978-79 and 1990-91. As new industries are gaining importance, there are bound to be changes in the proportion of R&D expenditure in different industries. The purpose of this table is to identify those industries which registered large proportionate changes during the period. It will be seen that the most significant increase was in fuels followed by metallurgical, transportation and industrial machinery. In contrast, there was a marked decline in the proportion of R&D expenditure in chemicals and defence. Some other industries which witnessed a marginal decline were agricultural machinery, electrical equipment, machine tools, fertilizers, drugs and pharmacauticals.

TABLE 3.9: **R&D Expenditure in Selected Industries as a Percentage of Total R&D Expenditure, 1978-79 and 1990-91**

Industries	1978-79		1990-91	
	R&D Exp. (Rs.crores)	%	R&D Exp. (Rs.crores)	%
Metallurgical	6.87	5.08	93.68	9.79
Fuels	1.48	1.10	73.05	7.63
Agricultural Machinery	2.94	2.17	10.85	1.13
Electrical Equipment	22.87	16.91	150.62	15.74
Machine Tools	2.27	1.68	12.03	1.26
Telecommunication	10.97	8.11	54.12	5.66
Transportation	6.76	5.00	73.26	7.66
Industrial Machinery	3.45	2.55	41.79	4.37
Fertilizers	4.27	3.15	25.23	2.64
Chemicals	18.73	13.85	72.96	7.63
Drugs & Pharmaceuticals	11.75	8.68	76.81	8.03
Defence Industries	21.85	16.16	113.49	11.86
Others	21.04	15.56	158.84	16.60
Total	135.25	100.00	956.73	100.00

An important indicator of R&D intensity among industries is the proportion of R&D expenditure to their sales. Table 3.10 shows R&D intensity for the three years, 1988-89 to 1990-91, for the industrial firms in the public and private sectors.

It will be seen that the overall R&D intensity has marginally declined from 0.67 in 1988-89 to 0.66 in 1990-91. A comparison of these figures for public and private sectors shows that in the public sector R&D intensity moved up from 0.56 to 0.58 during the three-year period while in the private sector it declined from 0.80 to 0.74. It becomes evident from these figures that the private sector industrial firms are not spending on R&D activity even what they used to spend in terms of sales in the earlier period.

Table 3.11 presents R&D intensity data for the two periods 1976-77 to 1978-79 and 1988-89 to 1990-91. The purpose of this table is to ascertain whether any significant change has taken place in R&D intensity during this period

TABLE 3.10: **R&D Intensity**

Year	Total R&D Exp. (Rs. crores)			Sales (Rs. crores)			R&D Exp. as % of sales		
	Public Sector	Private Sector	Total	Public Sector	Private Sector	Total	Public Sector	Private Sector	Total
1988-89	342	407	749	60767	50571	111338	0.56	0.80	0.67
1989-90	413	478	891	69336	61354	130690	0.60	0.78	0.68
1990-91	444	513	957	76140	69488	145628	0.58	0.74	0.66

TABLE 3.11: **R&D Intensity in Public and Private Sectors**
(R&D Expenditure as Percentage of Sales)

Year	Public Sector	Private Sector	Total
1976-77	0.65	0.71	0.69
1977-78	0.70	0.78	0.75
1978-79	0.98	0.84	0.90
overall	0.79	0.78	0.79
1988-89	0.56	0.80	0.69
1989-90	0.60	0.78	0.61
1990-91	0.58	0.74	0.66
overall	0.58	0.77	0.67

It will be seen from these figures that there has been a decline in R&D intensity both in the public and private sectors. In the private sector, the decline was relatively less. As a result, there was an overall decline from 0.79 to 0.67 during the period under reference. One would have expected that in a subsequent period R&D expenditure in relation to sales would be higher on account of perhaps greater awareness and realisation of the importance of R&D activity amongst industrial enterprises. But contrary to this expectation, the trend is reverse. What is distressing is that industrial firms are not even spending one rupee out of 100 rupees of sales on R&D activity. They spent 79 paise per 100 rupees of sales during the first three-year period, 1976-77 to 1978-79, which declined to only 67 paise during the subsequent period, 1988-89 to 1990-91. Table 3.11 indicates that industrial R&D has remained neglected in the country.

Since the number of industrial units engaged in R&D is different in public and private sectors, one way of comparison is to reduce R&D expenditure per industrial unit. This is attempted in Table 3.12. The data relate to six major industries in which R&D expenditure is usually high. As regards comparison between public and private sectors, one finds that in four industries viz., metallurgical, electronic and electrical equipments, telecommunication and chemicals (other than fertilizers), R&D expenditure in the private sector is extremely low as compared to that in the public sector. In case of drugs and pharmaceuticals, R&D expenditure per unit is highest as compared to other industry groups within the private sector. However, it is less than that in the public sector. It is only in industrial machinery industry, one finds that R&D expenditure in per unit was higher in the private sector than that in the public sector.

TABLE 3.12: R&D Expenditure per Industrial Unit in Selected Industries (1990-91)

(Rs. Lakhs)

Industries	Public Sector	Private Sector
Metallurgical Industries	274.02	34.00
Electronics & Electrical Equipments	244.27	44.57
Telecommunication	294.96	17.33
Industrial Machinery	14.15	49.41
Chemicals (other than fertilizers)	140.30	34.88
Drugs & Pharmaceuticals	82.68	70.19

As this stage, it may be worthwhile to compare R&D expenditure in the small scale and medium and large scale industries. This has been attempted in Table 3.13 which shows figures for selected industry groups. It is revealing that the differences in the magnitude of R&D expenditure are extremely wide between the two sectors. For example, in metallurgical industries a small scale unit spent merely Rs.9.03 lakhs in contrast to over Rs.1 crore in the medium and large sector. Likewise, one finds extremely wide differences in electronics and electrical equipment, telecommunication, chemicals and drug and pharmaceutical groups.

TABLE 3.13: R&D Expenditure per Unit in Small Scale and Large Scale Sectors (1990-91)

Industry Group	Small Scale Sector			Large Scale Sector		
	No. of Units	Total R & D exp. (Rs. lakhs)	R&D exp. per unit	No. of Units unit	Total R&D exp. (Rs. lakhs)	R&D exp. per unit
Metallurgical	9	158.68	7.63	83	9209.74	110.96
Electronics & Elec. Equipment	66	836.34	12.67	142	14226.06	100.18
Telecommunication	26	202.55	17.79	30	5209.92	173.66
Industrial Machinery	16	209.77	13.11	75	3969.30	52.92
Chemicals	46	395.17	8.60	136	6901.15	50.74
Drugs & Pharmaceuticals	25	309.53	12.38	83	7371.02	88.81
Food Processing	13	1145.91	88.15	20	1054.22	52.71

A number of cooperative research associations are also engaged in R&D activity. To mention a few prominent associations – Automotive Research Association of India, National Council for Cement and Building Materials, Tea Research Association, Indian Jute Industry's Research Association, Bombay Textile Research Association and Ahmedabad Textile Industry's Research Association. Table 3.14 presents data on R&D expenditure incurred by all these associations for the three years, 1988-89 to 1990-91. It will be seen that R&D expenditure steadily rose from Rs. 3347 crores in 1988-89 to Rs. 4186 crores in 1988-89. However, cooperative research associations spent a very small proportion of overall R&D expenditure in the country. In 1990-91 their R&D expenditure was mere 0.48 per cent of total R&D expenditure in India, which declined to 0.40 per cent in 1989-90 and recovered somewhat to 0.43 per cent in 1990-91.

TABLE 3.14: **R&D Expenditure by Cooperative Research Associations**

(Rs. crores)

	1988-89	1989-90	1990-91
1. Total R&D Expenditure	3347.26	3725.74	4186.43
2. R&D Expenditure by Cooperative Research Associations	15.72	14.87	18.49
3. 2 as % of 1	0.48	0.40	0.43

Since R&D activity is highly capital intensive industry, small enterprises are unable to engage themselves in R&D activity. To ensure that such enterprises are also benefited by technological improvements, it is necessary that cooperative research associations are more intensively involved in R&D activity.

Table 3.15 presents data on R&D indicators for a number of countries. It is evident from the figures given in this table that R&D expenditure in industrial economies ranged from 1.71 per cent to three per cent of the gross domestic product in 1986. India with 0.8 per cent was on the top amongst low-income and middle-income developing economies. But it must be borne in mind that this higher proportion is of relatively lower income as compared to industrially advanced countries.

TABLE 3.15: **R&D Indicators**

Countries	Applied R&D/ GDP (X 100)		Applied R&D/ Value Added (X 100)		Scientists & Engineers Engaged in R&D in 1986		Basic Science/ GDP (X 100)
	All Sectors		Agriculture		Total	Per 1,000 workers	1986
	1970	1986	1970	1986			
Industrial Economies							
United States	1.65	1.85	1.96	2.16	785,000	6.56	0.42
United Kingdom	1.56	1.71	3.95	5.27	86,500	3.32	0.31
France	1.58	1.94	0.78	1.52	72,889	3.09	0.46
Federal Republic of Germany	2.03	2.60	2.94	2.83	128,162	4.62	0.50
Japan	1.84	2.75	3.28	2.54	531,612	8.80	0.37
Centrally Planned Economies	2.60	3.00	0.75	1.00	—	—	—
Recently Industrialized Economies							
Spain	0.2	0.5	0.21	0.81	15,299	1.19	0.07
Greece	0.2	0.2	0.32	0.63	3,000	0.77	0.06
Portugal	0.2	0.4	0.89	0.61	3,475	0.71	0.08
Israel	1.1	2.5	2.93	4.47	3,350	2.32	0.90
Newly Industrialized Economies							
Korea, Republic of	0.5	1.8	0.38	0.56	32,117	2.05	0.19
Singapore	0.1	0.5	—	—	2,401	1.95	0.15
Middle-Income Developing Economies							
Venezuela	0.2	0.4	1.95	1.18	4,568	0.97	0.08
Argentina	0.5	0.4	0.68	0.44	10,500	0.87	0.08
Mexico	0.2	0.6	0.11	0.63	16,679	0.76	0.10
Brazil	0.2	0.7	0.50	0.95	32,508	0.75	0.06
Chile	0.1	0.4	0.89	1.21	1,600	0.43	0.10
Colombia	0.0	0.2	0.61	0.64	1,083	0.12	0.02
Turkey	0.1	0.2	0.44	0.41	7,747	0.49	0.04
Thailand	0.3	0.3	0.91	0.60	n/a	n/a	0.06
Egypt	0.8	0.2	0.39	0.40	19,939	1.61	0.04
Philippines	0.2	0.2	0.41	0.18	4,816	0.23	0.03
Low-Income Developing Economies							
Indonesia	0.1	0.3	0.29	0.45	24,895	0.45	0.06
Pakistan	0.2	0.3	0.05	0.31	9,325	0.41	0.03
Kenya	0.1	0.1	1.34	0.81	n/a	n/a	0.02
India	0.4	0.8	0.16	0.35	28,223	0.12	0.12
Bangladesh	0.1	0.2	0.15	0.34	n/a	n/a	0.20

A point worth emphasizing is that a large number (over 28 thousand) scientists and engineers were engaged in R&D activity in India. However, when this number is reduced in relation to 1000 workers, one finds that the figure is merely 0.12. In other words, only 12 scientists and engineers per 100,000 workers are engaged in R&D activity. In a number of other countries, the corresponding figure is much larger. Even in Indonesia and Pakistan, which also belong to the low-income developing economies as India, the corresponding figure was 0.45 and 0.41, respectively.

TABLE 3.16: **R&D Expenditure in Selected Countries**

Name of the Country	Year	R&D Exp. as % of GNP	Per capita R&D Exp. in U.S. $
India	1990	0.9	2.76
Australia	1987	1.3	153.85
Austria	1985	1.3	110.71
Brazil	1985	0.4	6.41
Canada	1987	1.4	216.06
Czechoslovakia	1988	4.5	177.43
Germany (F.R.G)	1987	2.3	523.98
France	1987	4.6	364.13
Italy	1987	1.2	157.64
Japan	1987	2.8	558.80
Sweden	1987	3.0	577.57
U.K.	1986	2.3	226.83
U.S.A.	1988	2.6	514.70
USSR	1988	6.2	218.63

Table 3.16 presents data on R&D expenditure in selected countries. As the figures do not relate to a common year, these are not strictly comparable. However, these data would give a broad idea of the relative R&D effort in different countries. It will be seen that in terms of per capita R&D expenditure, India occupied the lowest position in 1990 with a meagre sum of $ 2.76 in contrast to $ 577.57 in Sweeden. Even Brazil was spending more than India on R&D activity. The series on the per capita R&D expenditure in terms of U.S. $ shows a very disappointing picture of Indian R&D activity.

As regards R&D expenditure in proportion to GNP, one finds that while India is slightly better than Brazil, it is much lower than all the other countries. In 1990, India spent slightly less than one per cent of its GNP on R&D activity compared to 2.6 per cent in U.S.A., 2.3 per cent in U.K., 3 per cent in Sweden, 4.5 per cent in Czechoslovakia 4.6 per cent in France and 2.3 per cent in U.S.S.R. Thus one finds that if India is compared with other countries, its R&D activity has been at a very low ebb and disappointing.

Analysis of Patent Statistics

One of the measures used to determine the output gained from R&D expenditure is the patent statistics. This is not, however, the only measure of output available – one alternative measure could be the number of articles published in scientific and technical journals, but this measures the scale of inventive activity. Generally, patent statistics are used to measure the output of R&D activity. But, as certain results are not patentable, patent statistics do not fully show the output of scientific and technological activity. These can be regarded, in part, the measure of R&D activity. In the absence of any better indicator of research activity, patent statistics could be used for analysis. However, before we analyse patent statistics, we should be aware of two underlying assumptions in the use of such statistics. First, that the ratio of patents to inventions remains constant over time. This may or may not be true. For example, some industrial firms may like to keep their invention as a secret and as such may not get it patented. Another factor that may affect the ratio of patents to inventions is the change in the standards of patentability applied by the Patent Office. The second assumption is that the 'average' invention in any year is of equal importance to the 'average' invention in all other years. In other words, the distribution of patents by importance remains unchanged over the years. Since there is no evidence available to support these assumptions, one has to be very careful in analysing patent statistics.

Table 3.17 presents data on number of applications made for patents in force for the years 1976-77 to 1989-90. It will be seen from these statistics that the number of applications filed for the issue of patents by Indians has always remained far less than the corresponding figure for foreign applicants. As regards the number of patents sealed, one finds that patents issued to Indians was not even one-half of the number of patents issued to foreigners. Obviously, this gap has widened when we compare the number of patents in force as the latter is in a way a cumulative series including the patents issued earlier as well. The last two columns of this table show these figures. It will be seen that broadly the number of patents in force (Indian) was not even one-fourth of the corresponding number in respect of foreign applicants.

One point that becomes evident from all these figures is that for a vast country like India, inventions are very negligible. The number of patents has to increase significantly if the country has to make rapid stride in agricultural, industrial and other economic activities.

TABLE 3.17: **Growth of Patents in India**

Year	Apps. for patents made by		No. of patents sealed		No. of patents in force	
	Indians	Others	Indians	Foreign	Indians	Foreign
1976-77	1342	1762	928	1964	2746	19780
1977-78	1097	1773	657	1857	3065	19795
1978-79	1124	1808	281	499	2469	13966
1979-80	1055	1925	516	1657	2786	14474
1980-81	1159	1795	349	670	2757	14448
1981-82	1093	1896	421	936	3038	14892
1982-83	1135	1950	405	822	3329	15291
1983-84	1055	2090	340	980	3523	15726
1984-85	1001	2318	263	1206	3008	13162
1985-86	999	2527	451	1500	2549	10844
1986-87	983	2506	532	1594	2004	10059
1987-88	930	2527	588	1516	2150	10115
1988-89	1077	2521	795	2585	2584	11015
1989-90	1039	2622	519	1371	2468	10941

The Department of Science and Technology collected data not only on patents sealed but also on products developed, processes developed, import substitutes developed, design prototypes developed and consultancy services rendered by R&D institutions in different sectors. These data were collected through its national survey. Some of these data are shown in Table 3.18.

Table 3.18 has been reproduced from the DST's publication on Research and Development Statistics 1990-91. The DST has mentioned that the response from R&D institutions in respect of these statistics was poor and sometimes incomplete. It does not rule out the possibility of these data being cumulative rather than for an individual year 1990-91. Even so, one can get some broad indications from the Table 3.18.

TABLE 3.18: **R&D Output by Sector During 1989-90**

R&D Output	Central Sector	Public Sector	Private Sector	State Sector	Total
Patents sealed	193	37	215	0	445
Products developed	401	891	4342	77	5711
Process developed	339	172	1891	28	2430
Import substitute developed	287	970	3476	3	4736
Design prototypes developed	187	335	1393	33	1948
Consultancy Services rendered	4589	1172	1108	11446	18315

It will be seen from these figures that in respect of consultancy services, the state sector is overwhelmingly important which accounts for 62 per cent of total consultancy services. In contrast to this, in respect of all other heads of R&D output, the private sector has the major share. It accounts for 76 per cent of products developed and 78 per cent of processes developed. The contribution of the State sector in terms of these parameters is extremely negligible.

Concluding Remarks

The foregoing analysis of R&D activity brings out its shortcomings into sharp focus. Since the analysis was full of statistics, it seems worthwhile at this stage to sum up the major conclusions emerging from it. These are : (1) There was a spectacular increase in R&D expenditure during the period 1958-59 to 1991-92. However, when R&D expenditure is reduced as a proportion of national income, one finds that this rosy picture fades away. (2) Of the three sectors, the Central sector accounts for the largest R&D expenditure (79 per cent), followed by the private sector (13 per cent) and the State sector (8 per cent). Although there has been a decline in the Central sector over the years, it still continues to be overwhelmingly important. This indicates that industrial R&D in the private sector is at a very low level. (3) Industrial R&D expenditure accounted for 23 per cent of the total R&D expenditure. (4) Amongst the industries, the most significant increase in R&D expenditure was in fuels. In contrast, there was a marked decline in chemicals. (5) An overwhelmingly large number of units in private sector spend an extremely limited amount on R&D. Of the 983 units in the private sector, 56 per cent of the units spend less than Rs.20 lakhs on R&D. In the public sector, only 35 per cent of the total number of 155 units spend less than Rs. 20 lakhs. Further, proportionately larger number of units in the public sector spend very large sums of money Rs.5 crores or more in R&D in comparison with the units in the private sector. As the public sector units have more financial resources, such a situation is to be expected. (6) A distressing feature is that on the whole R&D intensity is extremely low in Indian industries. On an average, only 67 paise are spent on R&D out of every 100 rupees of sales effected in the industries. A comparison of the three-year period 1988-89 to 1990-91 with the earlier three-year period 1976-77 to 1978-79 shows a decline in R&D intensity from 79 paise to 67 paise for every 100 rupees of sales. One would have expected at least an increase in the latter period. (7) As was to be expected, there are very large differences between R&D expenditure in the small scale units and that in medium and large scale units. In certain industries, expenditure on R&D per unit in the large sector was 30 to 40 times more than the corresponding expenditure in the small sector. This obviously points out the need for cooperative research especially for the benefit of the small units. Although R&D expenditure by cooperative research associations has risen in 1990-91 as compared to the proceding year, it still constitutes mere 0.43 per cent of the total R&D expenditure. (8) A very large number (over 28 thousand) of scientists and engineers are engaged in R&D activity in India. In absolute terms, this number is certainly very high. However, when this number is related to workers, one finds that only 12 scientists and engineers per one lakh workers are engaged in R&D activity. Even some other low-income developing countries such as Indonesia and Pakistan have a much higher number of scientists and engineers. (9) An analysis of patent statistics shows that the number of applications filed for the issue of patents by Indians has always remained far behind the corresponding number pertaining to foreign applicants. This suggests that inventions are very negligible in a vast country such as India. This perhaps also shows that largely R&D activity in India is in regard to adapting imported technology to her requirement which obviously does not lead to far reaching innovations.

4

RESEARCH AND DEVELOPMENT IN SELECTED INDUSTRIAL ENTERPRISES

Introduction

The preceding chapter has dealt with R&D activity at the macro level, the main focus having been quantitative analysis. This chapter is devoted to R&D activity at the micro level. It describes R&D practices in selected enterprises. Obviously, in a limited space one cannot give an account of R&D practices of a large number of enterprises. The inclusion of an enterprise in this discussion does not mean that it is the most important in the concerned industry group. The selection was essentially influenced by the availability of authentic information.[1]

Bharat Heavy Electricals Limited[2]

Bharat Heavy Electricals Limited (BHEL) is one of the important enterprises which has laid considerable emphasis on R&D activity. At present it spends about two per cent of its sales on industrial R&D. In the preceding chapter, it was emphasized that R&D intensity in Indian industry was extremely low : on an average 66 paise were spent for every Rs. 100 of sales effected. Seen in this context, BHEL is far ahead in R&D intensity. It has the highest R&D intensity in India. However, it has achieved this position after 15 years of concerted effort. In 1983-84, it spent Rs.19 crores on R&D which has steadily risen to Rs.42.5 crores in 1989-90. This is the highest expenditure on R&D by any industrial enterprise in the country.

BHEL's R&D policy aims at achieving technological self-reliance through a judicious mix of in-house R&D and selective tie-ups with foreign companies. About 80 per cent of R&D expenditure relates to short-term projects which may yield within a period of five years.

The remaining 20 per cent of R&D expenditure is incurred on the development of the basic know-how or on long-term projects.

The basic approach adopted for R&D programmes can be summarised as follows:

- Most of projects to be identified by Product Managers based on business needs and operational problems.
- Thrust on few major projects where focus is on joint development between Corporate R&D and Units. Some of these are 800 KV transmission equipments, coal gasification and combustion, non-conventional energy systems, etc.
- Setting up and managing National R&D institutes in relevant areas such as Welding, Pollution Control, Ceramics, Transportation, Combustion, etc.
- Increased interaction with major customers on R&D projects for greater acceptance. Some examples are shunt and series compensation schemes, residual life measurement of power plant equipment and enhancing their service life.
- In-house R&D efforts to accelerate absorption, adaptation and improvement of technology obtained from collaborators.

The progress of all the R&D projects are monitored at Corporate level. A system for approval, monitoring and review of R&D projects has been devised which outlines the procedure for initiating, scrutiny, approval, monitoring and review of R&D projects undertaken by BHEL. During various stages of implementation of R&D projects, regular reviews of physical and financial progress are also made through a multi-disciplinary team. These reviews are very helpful in providing direction to the projects. However, if necessary, projects are also dropped on the basis of such reviews.

A point worth emphasizing is that BHEL has also taken up the responsibility of establishing national institutes with the assistance of United Nations Development Programme. Pollution Control Research Institute has been set up in Hardwar. It caters to several industrial units in solving their pollution problems.

National Organic Chemical Industries Limited (NOCIL)[3]

This write-up relates to the development of Phosphanidon/Dichloronos technology. These are insecticides with applications in rice/wheat/cereals and fruits/vegetables, respectively.

NOCIL first approached NRDC with an interest in technologies for these products. In 1986, it signed agreements with NRDC/RRLH and NRDC/RRLJ for Dichloronos and Phosphanidon, respectively. This was followed by intensive work at the Research Institutes as well as at NOCIL R&D.

A series of discussions were held between RRLH/RRLJ and NOCIL R&D to finalise the design basis. As a first step, basic engineering packages were prepared by RRLH and RRLJ for their respective technologies. These packages were subsequently merged into a single engineering package for the multi-purpose plant by NOCIL R&D. In 1987, a detailed engineering package was prepared and NOCIL commenced trial production in 1989.

NOCIL continued its experimental work during this period to get a better feel for process parameters and process control steps, develop vendors and define raw material specifications and identify further optimization opportunities.

It may be emphasized that during plant and process commissioning, NOCIL R&D and project personnel were actively involved. This team effort from manufacturing, project and R&D helped achieve successful commissioning.

This case clearly indicates as to how a concept has been converted into a physical product of considerable importance. S.G. Kane, the Manager, R&D, NOCIL attributes the following factors for the successful R&D activity with regard to the two products under reference :

1. Availability of sound basic package from research institute.
2. Strong in-house R&D for absorbing this technology with linkages to
   - research institutes
   - in-house project group
   - in-house manufacturing
3. Strong in-house project group capable of linking with detailed engineering contractors.
4. Willingness of management for risk taking inherent in commercialisation of new technology.

HINDALCO Industries Limited[4]

HINDALCO Industries Limited (previously known as Hindustan Aluminium Corporation Limited) was incorporated in the year 1958.

Today it is a leading integrated producer of Primary Aluminium in the country.

The company has never been complacent to changing technology. Production facilities and processes are being continuously expanded and modernized to keep pace with the latest technological developments elsewhere in the world.

HINDALCO's R&D Division has grown rapidly since its formation two decades ago. R&D Laboratory is equipped with latest scientific and analytical equipments and instruments for testing of materials. The pilot plant scale studies are undertaken to closely simulate commercial plant conditions.

The objectives of its R&D activity cover a wide spectrum from proposing and trying out new technologies with a view to optimising production processes and equipment performance to the enhancement of aluminium's role in the national economy. Its R&D department also interacts with various defence organisations, national laboratories and technical institutions for fundamental research. In addition, the company has laid considerable emphasis on energy conservation, reduction of manufacturing costs, import substitution and recovery of by-products in its R&D programmes. This is in conformity with the national priorities laid down by the Government of India.

The company has been able to strengthen its R&D activity on account of several factors. A major factor has been a close linkage with national laboratories and institutions for conducting fundamental studies in aluminium technology. Another factor is that it has provided adequate in-house R&D facilities to its research personnel. Yet another factor is that top management has always provided complete freedom to R&D personnel and tried to boost up their morale from time to time. Non-interference in day-to-day research and development work and existence of a congenial research environment have considerably contributed towards strengthening R&D activity of the company.

Lubrizol India Limited[5]

It is necessary for the success of R&D activity to have both forward and backward linkages with manufacturing and sales. A case in point is that of Lubrizol India Limited, Bombay. It is a company that manufactures chemical additives. It has accorded considerable imporatnce to R&D. It has tried to identify clear-cut, time bound, result oriented projects, keeping in view the basic national priorities. Over the years, it has developed its R&D strategy which is as follows:

- Practical goal directed research with horizon of short-term research
- Development of newer products keeping long-term objectives in view
- Trouble-shooting in manufacturing, having short-time frame and based on existing knowledge
- Strategic technical service (Technical Sales)
- Basic research to expand technology resources and technology innovation
- Coordination of forward and backward linkages with manufacturing and sales.

Through its own R&D efforts, the company has developed a range of polymeric additives which are now marketed by it.

In order to strengthen its in-house R&D, Lubrizol India Limited has identified certain measures. These are : (1) strengthening linkages between in-house R&D and manufacturing; (2) strengthening linkages between in-house R&D and national laboratories; (3) promotion of in-house R&D activities by interacting with other R&D centres of oil industry and OEMs.

The company has been able to increasingly indigenise additive manufacture as also utilize indigenous raw materials mainly because of its emphasis on its own R&D efforts. Its R&D has helped it in bringing in newer technologies. This apart, it has enabled the company to achieve maximum cost-effective operations which in turn have increased its profit without any increase in the price of its products.

Punjab Tractors Limited[6]

The original CMERI know-how covered a single tractor model, the 20-horsepower Swaraj 724. In the past 15 years, the Swaraj tractor line has multiplied into four basic tractor models ranging from the low-cost single-cylinder Economy Swaraj-720 to the highest 59 horsepower Swaraj-855. This product range is wider than the combined product line-up of the entire domestic tractor industry in size and price range. Swaraj R&D has also introduced the 100 horsepower Swaraj self-propelled harvester combine (1980) and Swaraj forklifts (1986). Both these products form substantial product lines for Swaraj today.

This spectacular progress of Swaraj R&D was on account of the following factors :

1. Self-confidence of top management in taking investment decisions on development, production and marketing of products based on in-house R&D. These investments for major products were invariably large.
2. Confidence in the entire team in its capabilities of making R&D a commercial success.
3. The habit of perseverance in the entire team to design and improve a product, till it met every customer need and desire.

Apart from these factors, Swaraj became customer-oriented. Sensitized customer-linkage became an all-pervasive part of Swaraj culture and made it totally market driven. High customer sensitivity, proven capability and confidence at product innovation to serve customer need coupled with marketing, enabled Swaraj to have a steady stream of new products.

It may be relevant to mention that within 15 years of background, Swaraj R&D is today at a stage when it can introduce three to four major products every year. Another major consequence of in-house R&D is the percolation of the innovative spirit in every aspect of the organisation: manufacturing approach and production processes, marketing, industrial relations and, in fact, total management. Experimentation with new products and progress through trial and error become a part and parcel of the entire organisation. Once the organisation is in this cycle of growth through innovation and evolution, even absorption of any new technology and build-up thereon becomes easier and faster.

The discussion so far related to large industrial enterprises. Normally small scale industrial (SSI) units are not in a position to undertake R&D on their own mainly because of financial constraints. However, there are certain units belonging to this group which have been giving considerable attention to this activity. As a result, they have gained considerably in terms of productivity and profitability. A case study of one such unit is given below.

Litex Electricals Private Limited[7]

This small unit has a work force of 46, including ten S&T personnel. Only two of the S&T personnel are deployed in S&T activity. The other eight S&T personnel spend 20 to 50 per cent of their time on different development projects.

The unit has set up a system of holding three different types of meetings in which new concepts are generated, scrutinized and followed up by product development. The first is engineering meeting. In a typical meeting, some 50 on-going products are reviewed by S&T personnel. These projects are classified into four groups : (a) new equipment development, (b) maintenance, (c) cost reduction, and (d) safety. The discussion of maintenance problem often leads to equipment modification. Each engineer works on 8 to 15 projects besides his/her regular assignment. The concerned engineer reviews the progress made on the project while others attending the meeting make suggestions and finally the future course of action is decided in consultation with the chairman of the meeting. At the end of the meeting new ideas are solicited from each engineer.

The second type of meeting is known as the product development meeting in which development programmes are reviewed by the participants. Development of new process and equipment is an integral part of product development.

The third type of meeting is the follow-up meeting. At least twice a week a senior executive and a manager (Production or Quality Control Manager) meet engineers individually in order to review the progress achieved in different tasks assigned to them.

It is interesting to find out that the company has made spectacular progress during the past seven years. (i) Its sales have increased at a compound rate of 43 per cent per annum. (ii) Its labour productivity (number of lamps produced per employee) has increased at a compound rate of 20 per cent per annum. (iii) Finally, the product range which was merely five at the beginning has increased to 95 lamps.

Some Generalisations

The preceding account of notable achievements made in selected industrial enterprises in the immediate past brings out factors contributing to their success in R&D activity. While some factors are exclusive to the concerned enterprises, there are others which seem to be existent in almost all of them. In this section, an attempt is made to identify these factors.

The first and foremost factor seems to be the existence of a strong in-house R&D centre/department within an individual enterprise. Successful units have not only set up R&D centres/departments but have also ensured that they have competent and dedicated persons to work on R&D projects.

Second, wherever national laboratories are engaged in similar type of work as an industrial enterprise, the R&D personnel of such an enterprise have not only kept themselves well-informed about the work of national laboratories but have had effective linkages with them. In fact, there are two types of linkages – (1) linkage between in-house R&D centre and the manufacturing division of an enterprise, and (2) linkage between in-house R&D centre and the national laboratories. Both the linkages were effective. This has enabled them to have optimal benefit in the event of utilization of a new process or product developed in a national laboratory.

Third, all success stories in R&D activity suggest that the concerned enterprises exercised great care in choosing their projects. In order to ensure successful R&D activity, the enterprises have to be clear in their corporate and R&D objectives and the economic environment in which they were operating. In a number of cases, research projects were identified by management on the basis of business needs and operational problems.

Fourth, spectacular progress in R&D was noticed in those enterprises which had set up a proper system of monitoring and review of R&D projects. Such monitoring and reviews enabled the enterprises to identify the reasons responsible for slow progress, if any, in R&D activity. The system also enabled them to provide the much needed direction to R&D projects right from their inception to their completion.

Fifth, the top management in all these enterprises was found to be liberal and appreciative of the role of R&D personnel. It provided them sufficient freedom to operate within an overall framework. In addition, it was found to be willing to undertake financial risk which was obviously inherent in commercialisation of new technology. Thus, the contribution of top management was very important as it kept R&D personnel free from any financial worries and uncertainties. They were sure that their project would not suffer for want of finance and that, if successful, its results would be implemented.

Speaking on the need for proper management of R&D, Raja Ramanna, former Chairman of the Atomic Energy Commission, Government of India, observes : "If one has to avoid obsolescence and repeated import of technology from abroad, we must have managemental system which will encourage originality and innovation. The failure of our R&D units in our industry, private and public, except for a few exceptions is a clear indication that managemental systems have failed because we have not taken into account the need for encouragement of originality, the upgrading of products and sustaining a class of workers who contribute to this aspect of an industry. At the moment people involved in R&D are given the lowest priority in a production system."[8]

Almost similar views are expressed by Abid Hussain when he says: "It is indeed sad commentary on our system that it ignores the technician, scientist and researcher and showers dignity and prestige to pen-pushers and to those who are farthest removed from production. Denigration of our technical men must be ended. Believe me, any management that does not assign high status and prestigious positions to its engineers and technicians, sooner or later comes to grief in a competitive world."[9]

These two observations made by two eminent persons, independently, at two different times should be an eye opener. Unless R&D people are given adequate freedom, recognition and their rightful place in an industrial unit, it is difficult to have major innovations from R&D activity.

So far we have enumerated the factors contributing to the successful completion of R&D projects. The researcher had discussions with some senior executives and officials. This has brought out certain aspects which need to be strengthened to derive maximum benefit from R&D activity. First, basic or fundamental research is hardly undertaken by enterprises. Their focus is on applied research leading to the development of new processes and products. While the emphasis has to be on the latter, basic or fundamental research should not be completely overlooked or else there would be no far-reaching innovations. Second, there should be far more awareness in regard to the productivity of R&D activity. A firm may spend a large amount on R&D and yet it may not reap commensurate benefit from it. Since there can be various indicators to assess the performance of R&D, it is desirable to develop overall standards or norms for evaluating R&D productivity. In the absence of a clear concept of R&D productivity and its measurement, it is no wonder that several enterprises do not evaluate productivity of their R&D effort. Finally, R&D activity should not be linked with manufacturing alone but should also be linked with marketing. There does not seem to be sufficient recognition of the market potential as an important factor for successful innovation. The actual linkage between R&D and marketing will depend on a number of factors. However, some broad guidelines can be followed in this regard.

Marketing aspect has, by and large, remained neglected by Indian enterprises. As a result, many findings have remained on paper and could not be commercially exploited mainly because of lack of market potential. It seems that R&D activity of research institutions is subject to this limitation in a greater measure than that of industrial firms. The importance of marketing has been dwelt at length in Chapter 2 while discussing major sources of innovation, as such it is not discussed here.

NOTES

1. The discussion is mostly based on the papers presented in the Fourth National Conference on In-house R&D in Industry held in New Delhi on the 22nd and 23rd November, 1990.
2. Based on a paper presented by K. Ramakrishnan, Director (Engg., R&D), BHEL in the Fourth National Conference on In-house R&D in Industry.
3. Based on a paper presented by S.G. Kane, Research & Development Manager, NOCIL , in the Fourth National Conference on In-house R&D in Industry.
4. Based on a paper presented by T.A. Venugopalan, Senior Vice-President (R&D), HINDALCO Industries Ltd., in the Fourth National Conference on In-house R&D in Industry.
5. Based on a paper presented by P.K. Rudra & K.A. Malik in the Fourth National Conference on In-house R&D in Industry.
6. Based on a paper presented by Chandra Mohan at the Third National Conference on In-house R&D in Industry.
7. Based on a paper presented by Avinash D. Kulkarni, Litex Electricals Pvt. Ltd., Pune, in the Fourth National Conference on In-house R&D in Industry.
8. Ramanna, Raja : "Management of R&D Institutions", Convocation address given at the Indian Institute of Management, Calcutta, on April 27, 1984.
9. From the convocation address delivered at the Indian Institute of Management, Calcutta, 1987. At that time Mr. Abid Hussain was a member of the Planning Commission, Government of India.

5

OPINION SURVEY OF R&D MANAGERS

Introduction

As was mentioned in Chapter 1, an opinion survey of R&D managers was conducted by the researcher. For this purpose, a detailed questionnaire was designed. The objectives of this survey were to ascertain the opinion of R&D managers on various aspects and to highlight major difficulties and problems that they face in carrying out their R&D activity.

This chapter is based on the responses received from R&D managers. An attempt is made to present their views on different aspects of R&D in addition to some factual data in a dispassionate manner.

Concessions and Facilities to R&D Units

To begin with, R&D managers were asked three interrelated questions namely (1) whether their organisation was registered with S&T department? (2) If yes, do they get any concession or facility from them? and (3) If yes, please specify the types of concessions or facilities. In response to the first question, all R&D managers answered in the affirmative. This is understandable as the questionnaire was mailed to only those units which were already registered with the Department of Science and Technology. As regards the second question, almost two-thirds of the respondents mentioned they did obtain concessions or facilities from the S&T Department for certain projects. Thus, two major benefits are available to R&D units: tax concessions and liberal imports of required equipment without payment of any duty. A particular respondent pointed out that DST compiled R&D statistics all over India and disseminates them to all registered R&D units in addition to holding seminars and conferences to get their views. He emphatically pointed out that no other help can be expected.

Time spent on R&D

Another question related to the time spent by R&D managers on different activities such as research, administration, consultation, library research, etc. The responses were extremely varied. To cite extreme cases, the minimum time spent on research was mere five per cent and the maximum was 70 per cent of the total time of R&D managers. Partly this difference was on account of the nature of the organisation where an R&D manager was employed. Thus in research institutes R&D managers generally devoted more time in research as compared to R&D managers in other enterprises.

In certain cases, the researcher came across a complaint from R&D managers that a large part of their time is spent on administration as a result of which they are left with hardly any time for research proper. However, the responses received in our opinion survey do not support this contention. In the majority of cases, the time spent on administration accounted for 20 to 30 per cent of the total time. Further, almost 60 per cent of the respondent – R&D managers opined that they would like to spend a little more time on technical duties as opposed to administration or non-technical duties.

Training Needs

A question was asked about the training needs. R&D managers were asked to indicate which of the following types of training would help them to do their job better : (a) technical training, (b) management training, (c) both technical and management training, and (d) neither management nor technical training. It is revealing that of the 32 R&D managers who responded to the opinion survey, as many as 17 were of the opinion that both technical and management training were needed to improve their R&D performance. This was followed by seven R&D managers who considered that management of R&D is an important activity wherein specialised training must be given. Some R&D managers emphasized the need for comprehensive training programmes for all R&D personnel. They were of the opinion that poor management of R&D projects does not allow the firms to have full benefits from such projects.

Types of Research

There are three types of research – basic research, applied research and development research. R&D managers were asked to indicate the relative share of each of the three types of research in their total R&D activity. As was to be expected, several enterprises were not at all engaged in basic research. Of the 32 R&D managers who responded to our survey, 16 managers (i.e. 50%) mentioned that they were not doing any basic research. Those who were engaged in basic research, indicated that it formed a very low proportion of their total R&D activity – 10 to 20 per cent only. In one case, basic research formed 50 per cent of the total R&D activity. The range in case of applied research was much wider, which varied from 5 per cent to 100 per cent while in case of development research it was from 10 to 90 per cent. On an average, one finds that R&D managers spent 52 per cent of their time on development research, 37 per cent on applied research and the remaining on basic research.

Objectives of R&D Activity

A question in the opinion survey was on the objectives of R&D activity. Several objectives were listed and R&D managers were asked to specify one or more of these objectives which were applicable to their R&D activity. In one case, R&D manager stated that none of the objectives contained in our question was applicable to his enterprise. He was emphatic in mentioning that the only objective relevant to his enterprise was to improve its innovative content and capabilities as a corporation. In yet another case, the R&D manager who belonged to a research institute was rather vague in his response and pointed out that the main objective of his institute was to remove poverty, unemployment and drudgery though it was not clear as to how this would be achieved. There were a few cases where R&D managers marked all the objectives specified in our question. However, the general indication was clearly in favour of a couple of objectives. The improvement of profitability, the improvement in the quality of the product and the improvement in the competitive position of the enterprise were the three most preferred objectives, in that order, amongst the R&D managers.

Use of Specialised Knowledge

A question contained in the opinion survey related to the use of specialised knowledge by R&D managers in their activity. They were asked to indicate how much specialised knowledge they normally use in R&D activity – considerable, moderate or extremely inadequate.

It is interesting to note that a little over 70 per cent of R&D managers thought that they used their specialised knowledge to a considerable extent in carrying out their day to day R&D activity. A little over 20 per cent of them used moderately their specialised knowledge. This probably shows that on the whole they are in a position to provide proper guidance and direction to their junior colleagues as the projects are either within their area of specialisation or very similar to their specialised field.

Selection of R&D Projects

Another important aspect on which the opinion of R&D managers was sought related to the selection of R&D projects. They were asked as to which of the following factors were considered by them, while selecting R&D projects and to indicate their priorities : (a) the researcher's interest, (b) practicability, (c) the urgency of the problem, (d) expected outcome, and (e) availability of resources.

On the basis of responses, one finds that 'expected outcome' was the most important factor. This was closely followed by 'the urgency of the problem'. Practicability of the research project was the third major factor in the selection of a project. Availability of resources and the researcher's interest, in that order were the least important considerations with R&D managers. It is rather surprising that R&D managers did not assign much importance to finance presumably because they normally had sufficient finances at their disposal and a categorical assurance from the top management that finance would be provided to them as and when they needed.

In the opinion survey, a question related to the involvement of staff in the selection of research projects. It is interesting to find out that barring one case which did not answer this question and one case in which it was clearly mentioned that staff was not consulted in the selection of a project, in all other cases R&D managers indicated that while deciding to work on any research project, they involved their research staff as well. Undoubtedly, this is a welcome feature in the management of R&D activity.

Procedure for Selecting R&D Projects

A question related to the procedure used for selecting research projects. A number of respondent managers just listed some important factors which guided them while choosing a particular research project. As against this, some managers understood the question in its proper sense and briefly mentioned the procedure adopted by them whenever they were to select research projects. The manager of a well-known organisation devoted to the dairy industry indicated that marketing federations identify a felt need of the consumer and refer the needs to its R&D department. It is then the responsibility of the R&D department to translate marketing ideas into saleable products. However, it was not made clear as to how the needs of the consumer were known – whether by informal discussions by a group of consumers or by undertaking a detailed study in this regard or by any other method. Another firm which is a leading industrial unit in the automobile industry mentioned that it first undertakes a detailed analysis of market before selecting any R&D project. This is perhaps one major factor that its products (especially the two-wheelers) are popular amongst the consumers. Some other firms have also been following more or less the same procedure. They all lay emphasis on market potential of the proposed new product. A firm has mentioned that it has a product based, applied research, largely application department. In that respect, consumer's interest plays a major role in selecting and designing a project.

A research association pertaining to the textile industry answered this question indicating its systematic approach. It first invites project proposals from senior staff. These proposals are then scrutinized in the R&D Committee in consultation with experts from outside. The proposals thus approved are placed before the Screening Committee for sponsorship. It has also mentioned that due weightage is given to projects regarding the possibility of transfer of output to industry.

An engineering firm has specified the following procedure for selecting research projects :

(i) Identify areas/particular problems requiring developmental work for company's anticipated future activities;
(ii) Formulate programme objective, schedule, budget and resource requirements; and
(iii) Select the project for implementation after judging its feasibility in terms of financial resources and manpower available.

Another firm which manufactures steel narrates the procedure as follows :

(i) Corporate plan and requirement for diversification.
(ii) Technological forecast as to emerging markets.
(iii) Short lead time for development and launching of the product.
(iv) Own interest to take up and optimism on product success in the market.

The foregoing discussion shows that different procedures are used by different companies while selecting R&D projects. No doubt, some procedures are more systematic than others. The companies which claim to follow systematic and detailed procedure in choosing their R&D projects are invariably found to be doing very well in the market and their products are popular amongst the consumers. It may also be emphasized that a large majority of the companies (almost two-thirds of the total), which are engaged in the manufacture of consumer products, do take into account the prospective demand for the proposed product before they commit themselves to the concerned project. Some of them involve themselves in detailed analysis and technological forecasting while a good number of them just satisfy them broadly that market prospects are quite good and the product will be well received. This discussion based on our survey confirms what has been said earlier in Chapter 2 with respect to foreign companies namely market potential is a major source of innovation.

Programme for Implementation

After the selection of the project has been made, the next major question is as to how the programme for its implementation is formulated. This information was sought by us from R&D managers in our survey. In this case, too, one finds several categories of responses. There were some sketchy responses which did not disclose much and some of these were rather vague. Some responses were routine-type indicating a more or less standardised procedure followed in the formulation of plans. There were only a few companies/organisations which were quite specific and mentioned adequately the practice they followed. Let us look into some of these responses.

A company mentioned that in the beginning it finds out whether work has already been done in the field for a similar project. Here, it takes into account all resources namely finance, human and technology. It then splits the entire project into suitable time frames.

Finally, it reviews the performance against the targets set earlier.

Another company of all-India fame first concerns itself with laboratory work in order to evolve or adopt suitable analytical methods. This is followed by the development of suitable processes based on pilot plant trials. The next stage is to assist engineering department in scale-up operations. Finally, it ensures that adequate resources (material, human and financial) are available.

An industry association belonging to one of the major industries observes that it assesses project work done every month through monthly and quarterly reports in the presence of the R&D Committee/panel of experts. Besides, seminars are arranged at periodic intervals where other staff members express their ideas. On completion of the project, a complete write-up is prepared. It also encourages the publication of research papers by its R&D personnel.

A company engaged in the manufacture of electronic items emphasizes that while selecting a particular prototype to be developed, it considers the present day demand and requirement of that system. Once it finalises the system whose model is to be prepared, its R&D personnel go through many reference books, journals, manuals and equipment systems. It then prepares the necessary flow chart, plan sheet, drawings, etc. Then each of the team members takes individual responsibility and tries to finish the job as per time schedule. Finally, the company assembles and tests the system for approval. More or less the same procedure is followed by some other companies belonging to different industries.

A steel manufacturing company formulates a three-year plan of its R&D activity by identifying projects. This is followed by a comprehensive annual plan, detailing budget and project execution schedule. Then individual project development schedules with resource requirements of manpower capacities, materials, etc. are finalised. Finally, key individuals are assigned to ensure satisfactory progress of different projects.

A company in the chemical industry first asks its research staff to undertake library work for finding new ideas/products. This is followed by (a) exploratory experiments, (b) lab-scale research work (c) scale-up to pilot plant, and finally (d) technology-transfer to manufacturing plant. It formulates time-bound programmes in all stages, specified above.

To generalise, we may say that not all responding companies adopt well-defined and systematic approach towards formulating plans for implementation of R&D projects. The companies which adopt a systematic approach, lay emphasis on varying aspects. However, a more common approach that seems to emerge starts with the study of relevant literature and library work, assessment of the finance, materials, and manpower available, splitting up of the project in suitable parts and their assignment to individuals, periodical reviews and finally integration of parts into a full-fledged outcome.

Monitoring of Projects

As regards monitoring of projects, it is revealing that only four out of 32 companies mentioned that they do not follow any monitoring of progress in their projects. There were two companies which indicated that they occasionally monitor their projects. In contrast, a large number of companies i.e. 27, accounting for about 81 per cent of responding companies follow a specific system to monitor the progress of their projects at periodic intervals.

As regards the procedure of monitoring, it varies from one company to another. Some companies hold meetings at frequent intervals to review the progress made during the specified period. The periodicity of such meetings varies – weekly, fortnightly, monthly and in some cases even quarterly. In such meetings, results are reviewed against time and cost so that necessary changes can be made if a project is going slow or if excessive expenditure has been incurred. Some companies use PERT/CPM charts in their monitoring efforts. Where the projects are quite ambitious and long-term, monitoring is not done so frequently. In such cases, half-yearly and annual reviews are undertaken to assess the progress made. It may be pointed out that a large number of companies seem to be extremely cautious in ensuring that projects are implemented in accordance with the time schedule and within the financial resources earmarked for them. In view of this, they invariably undertake periodical reviews of the projects so that corrective measures, if necessary, can be taken up before it is too late to do so.

Major Difficulties

In the opinion survey, an attempt was made to find out major difficulties faced by companies in undertaking their R&D activity. It is revealing that only two companies were categorical to say that they did not face any difficulty in their R&D activity. Another company in the public sector mentioned that while none of the difficulties specified in the questionnaire it faced, there was altogether a different problem with it. It said that while funds might be there to use, its R&D personnel had to spend almost one-half of their time competing with procedure and practice. As regards other companies, their responses indicated as follows :

Difficulties faced	*No. of companies*
Shortage of particular skills	14
Financial constraints	16
Shortage of raw materials	17
Government regulations	12
Indifferent attitude of management	5

It may be noted that the number of companies exceeds the total number covered in the survey. This is because a number of companies mentioned that they faced two or more difficulties. It will be seen that shortage of raw material was listed by the maximum number of companies. It was closely followed by financial constraint and shortage of particular skills. It is worth noticing that only five companies felt that management was not cooperative and its indifference created a bottleneck in their day to day R&D activity.

The next question was whether the company has ever dropped any R&D project without completing it. It is interesting to find that 17 companies mentioned that they never dropped any R&D project while 16 companies responded that they had to drop their R&D projects at times. Thus, the two groups are almost equal. As regards the reasons for dropping the project, one-half of these companies admitted that because of market being unattractive, they had to give up the project. This probably shows that some time after initiating the project, they must have undertaken a detailed study on marketing aspect and were convinced that the demand for the new product would not be sufficient to justify its commercial launching. This once again confirms our earlier conclusion that R&D and marketing have to be properly integrated before selecting a project.

Let us now briefly see some of the other responses in this regard. A computer manufacturing company suffered on account of non-availability of technical information as well as supporting software. Another company felt handicapped in continuing the project on account of high cost of imported equipment and raw materials. An engineering company which took up a project for the development of a new product, found to its dismay that there was a faster growth of technology in that industry. As a result, its project became superfluous. A soap manufacturing company had to give up the project due to lack of pilot plant facilities. This was further aggravated on account of the transfer of the project coordinating officer to another department. This reveals that sometimes deployment of senior people is erratic and there is no systematic personnel policy of the company in this respect. In yet another case relating to an electronics company, it laid the blame on the consumers. It mentioned that the prototypes were not accepted for manufacturing and commercial development as the customers changed their opinion subsequently. A research institute had to leave several projects mid-way on account of different factors of which finance was the most important. It was also very critical of arbitrary approach of the concerned funding agency.

R&D Personnel

The survey also sought information on the method of recruitment of R&D staff. Two questions were directed for this purpose. R&D managers were asked as to how they recruit research staff – (a) from the open market, and (b) within the organisation. The maximum number of responses (13) indicated that recruitment was made both from within and outside the organisation. This was closely followed by 12 responses favouring open market recruitment. In contrast, only six companies normally selected their research staff from within the organisation. One R&D manager said he did not have any authority in this regard and did not specify the normal practice followed by his organisation. Another organisation, being a research institute, normally appointed honorary experienced persons to undertake R&D work. One manager emphasized that while both the methods are used, the main difference is for routine type of jobs staff from within the organisation is chosen and for jobs requiring specialised research competence, selection is made from the open market.

R&D managers were also asked to specify which of the four considerations given in the questionnaire, they generally follow while selecting a researcher. The four considerations were : (a) technical competence, (b) length of experience, (c) training in foreign countries, and (d) standing within the organisation. An overwhelming number of responses (31) were in favour of technical competence. This was followed by 10 responses showing the length of experience as the most important consideration in the selection of research staff.

There were seven responses which favoured standing in the organisation as the most important consideration. It is interesting to find that foreign training elicited only three responses, indicating that it was not at all an important consideration before the senior R&D personnel at the time of selecting research staff. As in other cases, here too the total responses exceed the number in the sample.

R&D managers were also asked to indicate on the whole what quality of research personnel was found in their organisation. It is interesting to know that the last three categories (moderately poor, poor and extremely poor) drew blank. The maximum number of responses indicated their research staff as 'good'. This was followed by 'extremely good' and 'moderately good' each of these two categories had eight responses.

Another question related to any handicap felt by the organisation on account of shortage of research staff. Of the 33 R&D managers, 18 felt that they were really handicapped on account of shortage of research personnel, while 15 managers did not experience this shortcoming.

R&D managers who said that they felt handicapped on account of shortage of personnel, were asked to specify further as to what was the reason. Their responses were varied. But quite a few of R&D managers were of the opinion that they were forced to use qualified persons for administrative work in order to meet a long array of procedures. This resulted in actual shortage of research personnel. Some others opined that many scientists and engineers engaged in R&D projects lack motivation and no disciplinary action was possible to extract greater amount of work from them. This was a more serious handicap in large public sector enterprises. One R&D manager specified the lack of leadership as the root cause for slow progress in R&D activity. His reference was to the top management that it did not provide a high degree of leadership to R&D personnel. These were then some of the major factors which put hurdles in respect of the availability of right type of R&D personnel as also in building up a conducive environment for motivating them.

R&D managers were asked to indicate any incentives offered to R&D personnel for their superior quality of work. A number of incentives were listed in the questionnaire. In only two cases, R&D managers mentioned that no incentives of any type are offered to the research staff. It is interesting to note that this response was from the public sector enterprises. Amongst those enterprises which specified incentives, the most popular incentive was in the form of sufficient freedom to work. This was followed by better working conditions and freedom to publish research papers. A little over one-third of the enterprises mentioned higher salary, special reward for meritorious R&D work, security of job as the incentives offered by them.

Since the survey was addressed to R&D managers, it tried to collect information from these managers on the conditions which could induce them to leave their present company. As many as eight managers mentioned that no reason would induce them to leave their present company or organisation. Some of them were frank enough to say that as they are of an advanced age, they would like to retire from the present company. Some of these respondents started these companies or organisations and have identified themselves with them. An executive director of a research institute was very much devoted to his R&D activity. He mentioned: "This is my mission. I have refused top consultancy assignments from abroad and VIP posts in the country." Such persons are a rare breed, exclusively devoted to their research pursuits.

As regards the remaining respondents, one finds their responses as follows :

Conditions	*No. of respondents*
Higher salary	12
Improved working conditions	13
Better research facilities	12
Increased responsibility	8

The total of these figures exceeds the number of respondents as many of them mentioned more than one condition on which they may leave their present job. The first three conditions had more or less the same number of responses. It is worth mentioning that only 12 managers out of 33 would be induced to leave their present organisations on account of higher salary.

Summing Up

The foregoing analysis has dealt with some major aspects of R&D activity. It has primarily focused on the views of R&D managers on their work and the problems faced by them. They have also made certain suggestions which should be implemented to promote in-house industrial R&D in the country.

6

INSTITUTIONAL COLLABORATIONS IN RESEARCH AND DEVELOPMENT

Introduction

Before examining institutional collaborations in undertaking R&D, it may be worthwhile to know the organisation of R&D in India. There are various types of agencies that are engaged in R&D activity. A number of departments/organisations in the ministeries of the Government of India are involved in R&D activity in their respective fields. These are Department of Atomic Energy, Council of Scientific and Industrial Research, Defence Research and Development Organisation, Indian Council of Medical Research, Indian Council of Agricultural Research, Department of Space, Department of Science and Technology and Department of Electronics. Some of these organisations such as the Council of Scientific and Industrial Research have a number of affiliated institutes/laboratories, each devoted to a specialised field. At the State level, there are organisations/departments where research and development activity is carried out. Besides, many public sector undertakings have also started their own research and development. There are many research associations in different industries where R&D activity is carried out. There are institutions engaged in co-operative R&D activity. These are devoted to problems of common interest within an industry. To mention some of these – Automotive Research Association, South India Textile Research Association, Bombay Textile Research Association, Wool Research Association, Cement Research Institute, Indian Plywood Industries Research Association, Indian Rubber Manufacturers' Research Association, Silk and Art Silk Mills Research Association and the Tea Research Association. These associations are representative bodies of the concerned industries and are interested in such problems that may be of interest to a large number of units in the same industry. There are a host of industrial firms in the private sector which have their own R&D cells/departments where research and development activity is undertaken on the basis of priorities and relevance of the problem faced by them. There are IITs and universities too where research and development activity is carried out. To complete the list, there is the National Research Development Corporation, which had been set up specifically to promote commercial exploitation of inventions, patents and know-how, originating from various sources, especially from R&D institutions supported by government funds.

The chapter focuses on three aspects, viz. (i) collaboration between IITs and industry, (ii) collaboration between university and industry, and (iii) the role of NRDC.

Collaboration between IITs and Industry

The first phase of development of science and technology was the establishment of R&D infrastructure. As a result, the Institutes of Technology, on the model of MIT in the United States, were set up in India. The main issue here is how far the setting up of IITs has contributed to the improvement of technology in the country. In other words, have IITs accelerated the pace of R&D activity in India? In this connection, we draw heavily on the findings of the Review Committee which was set up in May 1983 by the President of India. The Committee was asked to review the work and progress of the five IITs located at Kharagpur, Bombay, Madras, Kanpur and Delhi. The Committee submitted its report in December 1986. We first deal with R&D activity undertaken in IITs and then with the linkage between these institutions and industry.

The Review Committee has found that about 20 per cent of the IIT graduates leave the country and that out of 80 per cent who remain in India, the majority of them take up management jobs for which they are not trained. Only a small minority of IIT graduates join the engineering sector or the R&D sector for which they are trained. The Committee has estimated that about 13 per cent of IIT graduates are engaged in Research and Development in India as compared to 22 per cent who migrate and are engaged in R&D in advanced countries. Another surprising and unhappy feature is that 25 per cent of IIT graduates seek employment in marketing and management where they are not in a position to utilize their technical knowledge.

These figures clearly indicate that R&D activity in India does not gain much from IIT graduates. Since the Government is keen to promote R&D activity in the country, it is necessary to know why IIT graduates are indifferent to R&D activity and how IITs can play a more effective role in promoting R&D activity in the country. These aspects are discussed below:

R&D Activity in IITs : The Committee has clearly observed that the research work pursued by the IITs did not have much impact in the country. While IITs take up a large number of research projects, almost all these are sponsored by Government departments. Very few research projects are sponsored by the industry although there are a number of industrial consultancy assignments.

One important reason for this unhappy situation is that industry is able to import turnkey projects. Such turnkey solutions prevent IITs to solve industrial problems and deliver a turnkey product to industry. What IITs can do is to offer research solutions to certain industrial problems. IITs obviously are unable to give a turnkey product. Since IITs have R&D infrastructure, industry should be encouraged to tap these facilities in the IITs. The Government may even provide suitable tax incentives to industry for sponsoring research studies in the IITs.

Coordination among Different Agencies

As was mentioned in the introduction to this chapter, there are a number of agencies that are either engaged in R&D activity on their own or are concerned with the promotion of R&D activity. There is a need for effective interaction amongst universities, IITs and the CSIR chain of national laboratories. It is desirable to have greater mobility of personnel from one institution to another. Thus, IITs Faculty may visit universities for short duration, university teachers may be deputed to national laboratories and R&D personnel in such laboratories may be invited by universities and IITs. A properly planned exchange of research personnel of these three types of institutions will not only be beneficial to the concerned persons but will also enrich the quality of R&D activity. Unfortunately, there are no institutional arrangements for exchange of personnel amongst these institutions. A major barrier has so far been that each type of institution regards itself supreme and wants to work in isolation. The time has come when this approach has to be discarded.

Industrial Foundation

In order to encourage collaboration between IITs and industry, the Review Committee has recommended the setting up of an Industrial Foundation in each IIT. The industry should sponsor its research and consultancy projects with the Industrial Foundation. Such a foundation should be authorised to accept industry projects, obtain funds to meet not only the cost of the projects but also to generate some profit. The Review Committee has suggested a number of functions of the Foundation. One of these is that the Foundation should be authorized by its charter to promote a company if it is convinced that it is necessary for strengthening industry-IIT linkage

The main focus of the Foundation should be to develop indigenous technology through R&D. The Foundation is also expected to offer expert advice to the DGTD and DOE particularly in respect of import of technology. In addition, it should explore the possibilities of collaboration with other agencies to bring about technology development in India.

Development of Entrepreneurship: Another measure recommended by the Review Committee is that IITs should encourage transliteration of their research results into an industry. This can be done if the Faculty who has successfully completed R&D starts an industrial unit. The Faculty may be granted sabbatical leave or extraordinary leave for this purpose in addition to the use of normal facilities that are available in the IITs. Such a measure would be especially beneficial in refining a new process or product pertaining to new Hi-Tech industries. Apart from Faculty, IITs should encourage their students to become entrepreneurs instead of looking for jobs as employees.

Industry-Research-Education Nexus : In order to extend the base of technology research in India, there must be movement of personnel from one institution to another. There are a number of excellent centres of research in the university system and CSIR chain of national laboratories. However, these institutions work in isolation. There should be greater mobility between these systems. This is possible if IITs and universities and national laboratories encourage their personnel to move from one system to another.

At present, there is no institutional arrangement for strengthening the movement amongst these institutions. It is imperative that the culture of working in isolation is done away with. IITs should be in a position to play an important role in breaking such an insularity.

Industry's Viewpoint

While industrial units are interested in establishing an effective linkage between IITs and themselves, they find that there are some genuine problems in this respect. First, industry feels that IITs mostly take up academic projects and are reluctant to study practical design problems. Second, even when IITs take up sponsored research projects from industry, they fail to complete the projects in time. In some cases there are considerable delays and the industry cannot afford to wait that long. Third, it has been experienced in some cases that there was no continuity. The IITs assigned the industry-sponsored projects to their post-graduate students who left the institutes before the projects were completed. This not only resulted in unnecessary delay in completion of the projects but also affected consistency in the approach to the problems. Fourth, whenever the industry has sponsored projects with IITs, it expects that the concerned IIT Faculty would have frequent visits to the concerned industry and meaningful discussions with industry executives. But this seldom happens. This is partly on account of the fact that IITs consider industry merely as a funding agency for sponsoring research projects and do not regard it as an equal partner in a joint effort. Fifth, it has been felt by industry that IITs do not like that the industry should review the progress of their work in respect of sponsored projects. Sixth, IITs do not seem to give adequate importance to research methodology as also to the documentation of the procedure used in a study.

IITs' Viewpoint

IITs, on the other hand, have a different viewpoint. This is summed up below:

First, industry uses IITs for testing the new products and hardly sponsors any substantial problem for research. Second, it does not encourage IITs Faculty to collaborate within the industry. Third, industry does not provide any scope for research in new and challenging areas though IITs are very much interested in taking up research in such areas. Fourth, IITs feel that industry goes for indiscriminate import of foreign technology. This should be avoided.

It will thus be seen that industry and IITs have very divergent views and as a result there is no effective linkage between them. It is extremely necessary to know clearly the role of industry and IITs – what each one can do and cannot do.

The Review Committee has made some important recommendations to promote linkage between industry and IITs. Some of its major recommendations are: First, the Government should provide some kind of incentive to those industrial units which sponsor projects with IITs. This would encourage industry to assign more problems for study to IITs than hitherto. Second, IITs should appoint well-qualified persons from industry as adjunct professors. Likewise, there should be some provision for compulsory sabbatical leave to IITs Faculty to go to industry for a fixed tenure. This would develop better understanding between the two types of institutions. Third, it is advisable to appoint joint guides for supervision of M.Tech. projects. Fourth, there should be frequent visits of senior executives and industrialists from industry to the IITs. Lectures by such people would help develop a better understanding between students and industry. Fifth, industry should be increasingly involved in the framing of syllabi and curricula in IITs. In this context, it is desirable to review the post-graduate programmes periodically so that they can be updated, if necessary. Such reviews can be undertaken once in two years. Sixth, the industry should assign live problems to IITs which, in turn, assign them to their M. Tech. and Doctoral students. Seventh, it is advisable that the industry should bear the entire cost of research. This would cut down delays in the completion of projects and also ensure continued interest of the industry in the research project. Eighth, senior professionals from industry should be increasingly associated with IITs as Visiting Faculty. They should share teaching work in their specialised areas. This would be beneficial to both IITs and industry and help develop linkage between them.

Collaboration between University and Industry

The present scenario of university-industry collaborations in India is not encouraging. First, there is a lack of mutual understanding, rather lack of mutual appreciation, between the academicians and industrialists/managers of the complementary nature of their individual fields of activities. Second, most of the research done in universities which have adequate infrastructure facilities, tends to be very academic and in those areas which are not relevant to industry. Third, the university teachers are seldom fully acquainted with the industrial set-up and the requirement of industry. They are not fully conversant with the practical approach to co-ordinate the inter-related aspects, such as financing, marketing, sales promotion etc. Fourth, it is held in some quarters that the creation of various national research laboratories under the CSIR and other agencies have adversely affected both teaching and research in Indian universities. This is because many talented teachers have left universities to join these national laboratories on account of higher emoluments and better facilities. Finally, it is felt that universities have extremely meagre funds. As such, they are unable to provide superior instruments and machineries to their laboratories for conducting advanced research useful to industry.

Having looked into the present scenario of university industry interactions, we now discuss some major aspects of collaboration between universities and industry. It may be noted that universities are not generally so well-equipped as the IITs, which are specialised institutions. As such, a number of observations made earlier in the context of IITs are not applicable when we discuss collaboration between university and industry.

For the sake of convenience, the different forms of interactions are divided into the following four major categories :

(1) General Research Support
(2) Cooperative Research
(3) Knowledge Transfer
(4) Technology Transfer

Table 6.1 presents a variety of interactions that have been observed in selected universities in a study done by the Association of Indian Universities.[1]

During the course of this study, a survey was undertaken and university teachers were contacted. There was consensus that there were no insurmountable barriers to joint university-industry research interactions. Some of the obstacles indicated by the university teachers are : pre-publication review requirements and restrictions on the dissemination of research findings, shortage of staff in university departments and scarcity of laboratory equipments. Table 6.2 presents the consolidated picture in this regard.

TABLE 6.1: **Types of University-Industry Interactions**

General Research Support	Cooperative Research Support	Knowledge Transfer	Technology
1. Monetary Gifts	Industry funded contact Research Specific to Research Programme of Project	Personnel exchange	Extension
2. Equipment Donation	Industry funded Research Fellowship	Mechanism for stimulate personnel interactions— Advisory Board, Seminars Speakers Programmes, Publication exchange	
3. Industrial Contributions	Govt. funded University/Industry Cooperative Research	Consultancy	
4. Industrial Endowed Chairs	Jointly owned or operated facilities and equipment	Adjunct professorship	
	Informal cooperative interaction co-authoring papers, equipment sharing, information sharing.	Industry's participation in the teaching process	
	Preparation of curriculum	Seminars and short-term courses	
	Industry funded medals		

Source : Same as in the preceding footnote.

TABLE 6.2: **Barriers and Constraints to University — Industry Interaction**

Types of Barriers	No. of Respondents	Percentage
1. Pre-publication Review Requirements	8	5.4
2. Information Dissemination Restrictions	14	9.3
3. Shortage of Staff	41	27.3
4. Scarcity of Lab. Equipments	37	24.7
5. Others	20	13.3
6. Mixed Responses	30	20.0
Total	150	100.0

Source : Same as for Table 6.1.

In the foregoing table, the term 'others' includes such barriers as difference between the objectives of universities and industries, lack of flexibility in university structure and decision-making policy of the universities. It will be seen from the figures given in Table 6.2 that shortage of staff was the most important barrier followed by scarcity of laboratory equipment. As many as 78 out of 150 respondents, accounting for 52 per cent of the total, opined that these two factors were extremely crucial.

There are no clear and formal collaborations between industry and universities. It is necessary to ensure greater interaction between them. A number of measures are suggested in this regard.

First, universities should help industry in the setting up of research units in industry. They should provide competent personnel to man such research units. Second, universities should themselves take up live problems from industry for advanced research. At present researches done in universities have very little practical utility to industry. Third, industry should provide finances to universities for research so that its problems can be studied well in the universities. This is the practice commonly followed by the U.S. industry. Fourth, it is necessary that universities must identify their thrust areas where they are exceptionally well-equipped and where they can take up any challenging problem from industry for further investigation. In deciding such thrust areas, universities should ensure that they are in conformity with national or regional priorities. Fifth, it has been observed that many industrial research projects done in universities cannot be properly completed unless final investigations are carried out at the plants. This, however, is not always possible. This apart, it may give rise to several other procedural problems. To overcome such difficulties, the U.G.C. or the Association of Indian Universities (AIU) and the industry associations may jointly develop a standard code of practice in this regard. Sixth, pilot plant centres in different regions of the country may be set up. Such centres should be well-equipped in their specific subject-areas and should be available for use both by the industry personnel and the university teachers. As such centres would have all the necessary equipment and other facilities, they may be in an ideal position to evaluate workability and economic feasibility of a process or plant. Seventh, universities should involve knowledgeable persons from industry in their Board of Studies and similar other forums. They should ensure that the courses prescribed are not devoid of practical problems. This would ensure that university courses are more in conformity with real world problems as well as they are up to date. Eighth, as in the case of IITs, universities should also depute their teachers to industry for short periods. Likewise, industry should send its senior personnel for teaching and research in universities. This would ensure greater involvement and continued interest between the two types of institutions. Ninth, industry should be far more liberal in offering fellowships to post-graduate students than hitherto. Such fellowships will enable students to take research problems that are relevant to industry. Tenth, it is advisable to encourage industrial consultancy among teachers provided they do not spend too much time on the same. For example, they may be allowed one day per week for such consultancy work. This would widen the perspective of university teachers who would have a better understanding and appreciation of problems faced by industry. It would also enable industry to utilize the specialised knowledge of university teachers. Eleventh, as many small industrial units are unable to take up projects on their own on account of their limited resources, universities should help them in this regard. They should make their laboratory and research facilities available to small units on moderate charges. Such facilities should be provided for specialised problems of small units and not for normal day to day problems faced by them. Twelfth, a suggestion made in some quarters for setting up visiting committees is worth implementation. Universities should set up visiting committees for their science and engineering departments. Such committees should have industrial R&D managers and senior teachers as their members. These committees may carefully examine the research programmes, industrial openings for post-graduate students, etc.

It is hoped that if these measures are properly carried out, they would bring about more effective collaboration between industry and university. This, in turn, would contribute to R&D activity.

The Role of National Research Development Corporation[2]

So far the discussion was confined to IITs and universities. In this section, we now discuss the National Research Development Corporation (NRDC), a Government of India enterprise set up as a non-profit organisation in December 1953. The major objectives of NRDC are :

- Development and commercialisation of laboratory know-how
- Promotion and commercialisation of inventions

- Development and promotion of rural technology
- Export of technology
- Dissemination of information on technology transfer

The NRDC is engaged in a number of activities which are briefly discussed below :

Transfer of Technology: The NRDC has formal licensing arrangements for commercialising the know-how developed in R&D laboratories of major R&D organisations, research institutions of Central and State Governments, Industrial Research Associations, Institutions of Higher Learning and public sector and private sector industrial units, etc. The know-how is released to industry usually on payment of premium and royalty on sales. Know-how is also made available on a lump sum payment in lieu of the royalty and premium. Over the years the NRDC has become the model national technology transfer organisation in the country.

The NRDC has set up a Centre for Technology Transfer (CTT) for the development and transfer of technology in the country. The CTT works in close liaison with the Regional Centre for Technology Transfer, Bangalore, set up by the Economic and Social Commission of the Asia and Pacific (ESCAP).

Developmental Projects: The NRDC also puts up pilot plants, developmental and demonstration units in order to make the laboratory know-how suitable to industry for commercial exploitation. Ordinarily this is done in collaboration with industry. R&D institutions which develop the know-how are closely associated with such projects.

Equity Participation: The NRDC has a scheme to participate up to 26 per cent in the equity capital of companies exclusively set up for the commercialisation of NRDC technologies.

Horizontal Transfer of Technology: A scheme for horizontal transfer of technology exists to minimise repetitive import of the same technology. Under this scheme the NRDC helps the transfer of technologies from established organisations to new units.

Export of Technology: As most of the technologies available with the NRDC are less capital intensive, they are more suitable for developing countries. The NRDC has sold technologies to industry in different countries such as Philippines, Malaysia, Nepal, U.K. and U.S.A.

Invention Promotion: The NRDC has a scheme for promoting the inventive talent in the unorganised sector of R&D. Under this scheme it gives awards up to Rs. 10,000 for meritorious inventions. In addition, it provides financial assistance to inventors for patenting and building of prototypes. These awards are announced on the Republic Day and the Independence Day each year.

Conducting Training Programme: The NRDC conducts training programmes for R&D scientists/industry and entrepreneurs in the areas of patents and technology transfer, for the benefit of persons in both industry and research institutions.

Organising Exhibitions: The NRDC also organises technology licensing and project exports based on indigenous technologies. Such exhibitions are organised both in India and abroad.

The NRDC brings out a number of publications which are listed below :

Name of Publication	*Periodicity*
1. NRDC Processes	Half-yearly
2. Preliminary Technical Notes	As and when necessary
3. Market Studies and Feasibility Reports	As and when necessary
4. Processes in Production	Annual
5. Invention Intelligence	Monthly
6. Awishkar (Hindi)	Monthly

The NRDC is a repository of technologies developed in India. It acts as a bridge between research organisations and entrepreneurs. In the following paragraphs, an attempt is made to broadly evaluate its activities.

Table 6.3 presents data on the working of the NRDC for the years 1983 to 1992. It will be seen from the figures given in this table that the number of processes assigned had declined in the earlier years but it has shown a modest increase in recent years. The number of agreements executed has considerably declined from 129 in 1987-88 to 73 in 1991-92. One also finds that only a few processes

TABLE 6.3: NRDC's Performance 1983-92

(in Rs. Lakhs)

Year		Ending 31st March									
		1983	1984	1985	1986	1987	1988	1989	1990	1991	1992
Processes Assigned	Nos.	28	25	17	22	34	36	40	40	42	49
Agreements Executes	Nos.	120	136	138	140	119	129	101	92	78	73
Processes gone into Commercial Production	Nos.	11	5	5	4	13	10	4	10	4	5
Gross Royalty	Rs.	72.32	85.63	69.31	67.63	49.99	38.08	45.67	66.76	65.44	93.85
Gross Premia	Rs.	32.90	20.52	16.62	20.40	49.95	40.00	52.26	43.00	58.93	96.00
Other Income	Rs.	29.37	35.02	38.11	43.91	45.33	67.66	68.49	80.48	121.45	108.39
Grants-in-Aid received from Govt. of India	Rs.	23.00	25.48	18.00	32.00	20.00	20.00	35.00	42.00	47.15	60.79
Share of Research Institutions on A/c of Royalty and Premia	Rs.	73.70	74.29	60.13	61.67	69.61	53.68	67.87	75.56	80.56	125.51
Interest payment to Govt. of India	Rs.	10.65	12.34	15.46	16.94	16.32	13.88	12.40	10.65	8.43	5.80
Surplus before Tax	Rs.	5.09	2.71	3.90	2.55	6.51	22.83	25.09	21.71	63.67	68.44

Source : Annual Report of the NRDC, 1991-92.

went into commercial production each year. Despite these trends, the NRDC's income in terms of gross royalty and gross premia has increased from Rs. 1.2 crores in 1990-91 to an all-time high figure of Rs. 1.9 crores in 1991-92. The NRDC has been trying its best to widen its technology portfolio. According to its latest report, some leading private sector companies having in-house R&D centres recognised by the Department of Scientific & Industrial Research entered into MOUs with NRDC whereby they agreed to assign to NRDC technologies developed by them for licensing and commercialisation by it.

The NRDC has started providing market information along with the technical know-how licensed so as to make the techno-commercial 'package' more complete and to enhance the quantum of revenue realised from licensing. In order to achieve this, the NRDC has started commissioning professional market survey agencies to undertake time-hound market surveys on some of the major technologies in its technology portfolio. This new approach was introduced in 1986-87 and according to its Managing Director it has improved the results. Despite this, one finds that the NRDC's performance is rather mixed one – in some spheres it has been very good, while in others not so good. Its performance can be considerably improved if the suggestions, given below, are implemented.

A point worth emphasizing is that sufficient funds are not available to disseminate the results of R&D to prospective users. While national laboratories get grants from the government for R&D projects, no funds are made available to popularise R&D results. The Managing Director with whom this researcher discussed the role of the NRDC also pointed out this lacuna. He emphasized that even in developed countries larger funds are earmarked for dissemination of R&D results as compared to actual expenditure on R&D. The NRDC feels handicapped on account of paucity of funds.

Another suggestion to improve the working of the NRDC is that it must be enlarged. At present it has a very limited staff which cannot do justice with the objectives it has been assigned. Since our country is very large and as we have a widely diversified industrial structure, it is necessary that the NRDC must be expanded in terms of staff. With its present size and composition, the NRDC is unable to make any significant contribution to R&D activity.

Further, the NRDC should be directed to assume a wider and more responsive role than hitherto. In order to overcome hesitancy of industrial firms in regard to R&D activity, the NRDC can start pilot plants. After the plant has been in operation for some time on trial basis, it may be sold out to entrepreneurs who will then be willing to invest in it.

Finally, a criticism that has generally been made regarding the working of the NRDC is that in respect of new indigenous technologies it not only insists on long lease period but high percentage of royalty as well. As the technology is changing fast, it would be advisable to reduce the lease period. It would also be appropriate if royalty rates are reduced so that there may be greater response for the adoption of new indigenous technologies by industrial units.

Concluding Remarks

The discussion contained in this chapter brings out the following major conclusions :

1. As regards the IITs, time has come to have a critical look at the various courses imparted by them. There appears to be a genuine need to diversify the courses and bring them up to date. This apart, IITs should be concerned with the alarming rate of brain drain from India. Steps should be taken to reduce brain drain so that the country can be benefited. The Government of India and the IITs should jointly look into this problem.
2. IITs take very few research projects sponsored by the industry. This is indicative of poor linkage between IITs and industry. There is an imperative need for establishing a permanent unit linking the IITs and their nucleus with industry. As suggested by the Review Committee on IITs, an Industrial Foundation should be set up in each IIT for this purpose. Such a Foundation should focus its work on the development of indigenous technology. It may also advise the government departments such as the DGTD and DOE on the import of technology.
3. As regards collaboration between industry and universities, one finds that the latter are generally indifferent to the needs of the former. In order to ensure a meaningful collaboration between them, several steps are called for. To mention a few :
   (a) There should be exchange of research personnel in

industry and universities. Industry people should be encouraged to undertake advanced research under the guidance of teachers in the universities. (b) Teachers from universities should be given leave to take up short assignments in industry. Similarly industry personnel should be allowed to take up teaching assignment in universities for short periods. (c) Both industry and universities should take up some research projects jointly on the basis of their expertise in identical or similar areas. (d) Industry should provide financial support to universities for taking up research in selected areas. (e) Industry should also encourage some brilliant students at the post-graduate level to take up projects in which it is interested. Such students should be given adequate financial support. (f) Universities should provide refresher or retraining courses to technical staff of the industry so that they are upto date in their specialised areas.

4. The institutional collaboration in R&D activity is extremely inadequate, sporadic and loose. While the country has a good number of national laboratories under the CSIR, their research results do not benefit industrial units much. This is partly on account of the fact that the laboratories decide their R&D projects regardless of the needs of the industry. There should be greater and more effective collaboration between various institutions and industrial units in this regard.
5. The NRDC should strengthen its efforts in disseminating the results of R&D to industry. As the needs of a vast country like India are really on a large scale, it is advisable to strengthen the NRDC both in terms of finances and manpower. Further, the NRDC should lay far more emphasis in reaching out to prospective small scale entrepreneurs who would be interested in using the products or processes developed in national laboratories or other institutions. It is also desirable to reorganise the NRDC so that it is run efficiently and not like a government department.

NOTES

1. Association of Indian Universities : *University-Industry Interaction - Exploring Areas and Forms of Collaboration*, New Delhi, 1990 (mimeographed).
2 Based on the brochure brought out by the NRDC and the annual report for 1991-92.

7

TECHNOLOGY POLICY

Introduction

In this chapter, we discuss the role of the Government in augmenting R&D activity in India. Many policy-makers believe that the Government should adopt various measures with a view to increasing investment in research and development. The chapter first gives a brief account of incentives offered by the Government to industrial enterprises in India. It then goes beyond R&D incentives and focuses on technology policy in India. At the end, certain suggestions are made so that technology policy may become more conducive to innovative activity in Indian industry.

Incentives in India

The Department of Scientific and Industrial Research (DSIR) operates a scheme for granting recognition to in-house R&D units in industrial enterprises as also research and development laboratories. At present there are over 1200 in-house R&D units recognised by the DSIR. A broad sectorwise break-up of the recognised R&D units is as below :

Chemical & Allied Industries	...	375
Electrical & Electronics Industries	...	275
Mechanical Industries	...	225
Processing Industries	...	250
Agro Industries and Others	...	75

A major objective of granting recognition to in-house R&D units is to provide them liberalised import facilities so that they can import equipment, components, raw materials, etc. needed to carry out R&D activity properly. The DSIR grants recognition normally for a period of three years. This is renewable on application by the concerned unit.

The DSIR has instituted some annual awards for in-house R&D units for their outstanding achievements in the field of industrial research. This scheme has been in operation since 1957. The awards are in the form of medals or shields along with citations given to industrial R&D units for a particular year. It appears that the scheme has been very well received by in-house R&D units and it has encouraged several units to excel in their R&D activity and to bring about improvement in technology in their respective fields.

There are a number of schemes[1] under which different types of incentives are provided to R&D units, national laboratories and similar other institutions. The purpose of such incentives is to encourage the development of indigenous technology as also the adaptation of imported technology. A list of these incentives is given in Appendix II.

It has been observed that some enterprises take undue advantage of incentive schemes even though they are not genuinely interested in R&D activity. Thus, incentive schemes have been misused. It is, therefore, necessary to undertake a detailed review of all these incentives and to make necessary changes so that their misuse can be avoided. This apart, the Government policy at present lays emphasis on R&D expenditure and not on the outcome of R&D activity. One may spend a large amount on R&D and yet the result of such an activity may be very poor or meagre.

It should be emphasized that R&D is only an input and not an output. As R&D expenditure increases, it does not necessarily mean that technological advance has taken place. On account of this there is a clear case for standardizing the techniques of measuring the outcome of R&D activity. As far as possible, incentives should be related to the output of R&D.

It is our considered opinion that in the present state of India's development, incentives for R&D are very necessary. Without proper and varied incentives, R&D in India would continue to remain at a low level. The Government has to play a significant role in this regard. It has to devise new fiscal and other incentives that may encourage hitherto indifferent industrial units to take up in-house

R&D. But such incentives should be introduced after careful planning as also after a comprehensive study on the evaluation of existing incentive schemes.

We now turn to wider issues influencing R&D activity. The different incentive schemes for R&D constitute only a part of an overall technology policy. As such it seems worthwhile to look into technology policy in a wider perspective. In passing it may be mentioned that the first concerted effort by the Government of India for the preparation of a comprehensive Science and Technology plan was made in the Fifth Plan. The National Committee on Science and Technology (NCST) was set up for this purpose. Since we are interested in the policy aspects, we shall not go into administrative and procedural aspects of science and technology plans and policies.

Aims of Technology Policy in India[2]

The Government of India has laid down that the aims of its technology policy are to :

(a) attain technological competence and self-reliance, to reduce vulnerability, particularly in strategic and critical areas, making the maximum use of indigenous resources;
(b) provide the maximum gainful and satisfying employment to all strata of society, with emphasis on the employment of women and weaker sections of society;
(c) use traditional skills and capabilities, making them commercially competitive;
(d) ensure the correct mix between mass production technologies and production by the masses;
(e) ensure maximum development with minimum capital outlay;
(f) identify obsolescence of technology in use and arrange for modernization of both equipment and technology;
(g) develop technologies which are internationally competitive, particularly those with export potential;
(h) improve production speedily through greater efficiency and fuller utilization of existing capabilities, and enhance the quality and reliability of performance and output;
(i) reduce demands on energy, particularly energy from non-renewable sources;
(j) ensure harmony with environment, preserve the ecological balance and improve the quality of the habitat; and

(k) recycle waste material and make full utilization of by-products.

The foregoing aims clearly indicate that the Government wants to have a comprehensive technology policy with priority areas for technological development spelt out. The basic objectives of its technology policy are undoubtedly to (a) develop indigenous technology and (b) absorb and adapt imported technology in accordance with national priorities and resources. As regards the development of indigenous technology, some discussion has already taken place earlier. As such, we now turn to the import of technology.

Sources of Imported Technology

The sources of imported technology are :

1. Subsidiaries and branches of foreign firms with explicit and implicit knowhow arrangement.
2. Joint ventures with minority foreign capital and knowhow contracts.
3. Turn-key and "product-in-hand" arrangements but without equity.
4. Straight knowhow licensing contracts with payments in cash or kind.
5. Engineering consultants for project design.
6. Co-product or sub-contracting.
7. Inter-governmental cooperation and technical assistance from international organisations.

Since there are several sources of importing technology, it is necessary to select one or more source with great care on the basis of cost, convenience, consistency with the national policy and objectives, etc.

The Government of India has spelt out some major considerations regarding the import of technology. To begin with, the import of technology will continue to be allowed on a selective basis. Each case will be examined on the basis of such factors as the need for importing technology, non-existence of that technology in the country and the time taken to generate the technology would delay the achievement of development targets. Second, the government may identify and notify areas of high national priority wherein procedures for the import of technology may be simplified. Third, there should be a firm commitment for absorption, adaption and subsequent development of imported know-how through adequate investment in R&D on the part of importers of technology.

Some Comments on the Technology Policy

According to some authors, the technology policy pursued by the Government of India has been very restrictive. As a result, the Indian industry is subjected to technological obsolescence. This view holds that the policy has denied the use of imported technology which is modern technological without creating conditions conducive for generation of indigenous technology. This apart, imported technology and indigenous technology are not necessarily substitutes. Desai[3] holds the view that restrictions on the import of technology do not produce import-replacing technology. More liberal technology imports would channel indigenous R&D in those areas where either imported technology is not available or accessible or where returns are high.

Another observation made by Desai that needs to be emphasized is that the Government's technology policy should shift its emphasis from regulating the import of technology to encouraging the diffusion of all technology, local and foreign, in the country. It may be pointed out in this regard that the Technology Policy statement does mention that special efforts are needed for the diffusion of technology including horizontal transfer, technological support from large units to ancillaries, technology inputs to small units, etc. Diffusion of technology will enable the industries to be more efficient. Further, technology imports influence and are in turn influenced by domestic market structures. As suggested by Desai that the Government should be more neutral between State-owned and private firms, large and small firms, efficient and inefficient firms, if imported technology is to be more fully utilized.[4]

It may also be emphasized that the impact of foreign collaborations is different in different industrial units. Some units have progressively developed their own R&D and capacity for innovation while others in the same industry have become increasingly dependent on foreign technology. It is not clear as to what factors are responsible for inter-firm differences in regard to technological adaptations.

Technology Information[5]

An important pre-requisite for the appropriate choice of technologies is the existence of a comprehensive system of collection and analysis of relevant technological information. Realising the importance of information on technology, the Ministry of Industry and the National Informatics Centre are jointly developing the Indian Industrial Information System, involving the standardisation of format/questionnaire, software and as far as possible hardware.

In this connection, it is necessary to identify specific needs of different types of end-users of technology information. There are three major categories of end-users namely government and decision-making bodies, promotional bodies and enterprises. It is necessary to devise a proper system of consolidating the technology information from the micro level to the macro level.

As information is needed not only for the understanding of current status but also for anticipating future technology, it is necessary to set up a strong base for technological forecasting, information analysis, R&D management, etc. In fact, there is a need to have proper coordination between the industrial policy and the industry information policy. Similarly, there should be effective linkage between information policy and technology policy. Such linkages will enable an enterprise to choose appropriate technology in most beneficial terms.

Since technological changes are taking place in the world, it is necessary for developing countries such as India to overcome past deficiencies and to be aware of the emerging situation. It should be fully aware of the possible consequences of technological advances so that adverse consequences can be minimised and the benefits can be maximised. This suggests that there should be some mechanism for forecasting, monitoring and assessing technological trends. Such a mechanism should also indicate the possible implications of technological advances on social and economic development of the country. This would facilitate in formulating an appropriate technology policy. In this connection, the UNIDO secretariat has launched a series of review of global technology trends. Needless to say, India should draw upon these studies which give particular attention to the changing international technology market structure in newer fields such as genetic engineering, bio-technology, telecommunications, microelectronics, etc. In these newer areas, international cooperation is very necessary if a country is not to be lagged behind. As such, India cannot afford to remain aloof and unconcerned from the changing international technology market.

Development of Human Resources

At this stage, it may be mentioned that an important criterion in the choice of technology should be its potential impact on employment. In addition, technology policy should eventually lead to the development of human resources. It is necessary to increase facilities in the general science and technology in universities and research institutions. At the same time, the pressure for increasing intake of science and engineering students should be checked so that quality of education is not diluted. Universities must be restored to their proper image as centres of higher learning and research. This and other related aspects have been discussed earlier in the chapter on Institutional Collaborations.

Patterns of Government Intervention[6]

Before closing this chapter, let us briefly look into the approaches of different countries towards technology. The governments in different countries have adopted different approaches to technology policy. Some authors have attempted to classify different policies into particular categories. We give below the highlights of two such studies.

Rothwell[7] has studied policies on industrial innovation in six countries – Canada, Japan, the Netherlands, Sweden, the U.K. and the U.S. According to him, there are three major differences in the approaches to technology policy in these six countries:

1. Countries have used different tools or policy instruments. While the U.S. and the U.K. policy aims at creating a favourable climate for technological development, Canada, Japan, the Netherlands lay more emphasis on the provision of financial and technical assistance, including the creation of infrastructure.
2. Countries such as Japan have clear and long-term strategies towards technological change unlike others such as the U.S. which have provided complete freedom to individual companies in choosing technology.
3. In some countries, government intervention is viewed as a

major part of a process of indicative planning in contrast to those where industrial innovation policy is considered just one part of general economic policy which aims at creating a favourable climate for industrial development.

Eragas[8] uses altogether a different approach in classifying countries in terms of their technology policies. He classifies the countries into three categories :

1. 'Mission-oriented' countries (U.K., U.S., France)which employ science in a big manner to meet big problems. Such countries lay emphasis on high-technology research. In such countries, government spends far more on defence R&D.
2. 'Diffusion-oriented' countries (Germany, Switzerland and Sweden) lay emphasis on the diffusion of new technology among a large number of industrial units. For this purpose, they provide suitable education, product standardization and encourage cooperative research.
3. The third category consists of only one country namely Japan which has used coordinated efforts to achieve national technological objectives. At the same time, Japan ensures the supply of innovation-related public goods so that the process of technological advance can be speeded up.

It may be mentioned that Japan has been handling very different situations in its post-war development. First, it was engaged in an intensive technology catch-up phase (1950-69) to bring itself at par with the industrially advanced countries of the world. This phase was characterized by more direct control over technology import controls and the use of capital as a lever for directing industrial development to key technology sectors. This phase was followed by an intermediate period (1970-80) of a more independent development. During this period, some of the government laboratories played a major role in upgrading of industrial technologies. Now, in the present phase (since 1981), Japan is engaged in laying the foundation for its own and original development of new technologies. For this purpose, Japan no longer used its traditional direct and regulatory policy instruments, instead it uses indicative and indirect measures to promote long-term basic research. It has also launched programmes to enlist the private companies in joint basic research.

In the concluding remarks in his study, Jon Sigurdson[9] observes that while several developing countries – including India, China, Brazil and Mexico – have achieved a good degree of industrialisation, they lack in dynamic development as compared to already industrialized countries. The author attributes a number of factors to this situation. First, the Government has excessively directed and controlled the industrialization process. Second, partly as a consequence the competition among companies has been stifled. Third, there has been hardly any realisation that industrial processes and products need to be constantly upgraded so that production cost can be reduced and the competitiveness of indigenous products *vis-a-vis* foreign products can be maintained.

India must draw a lesson from Japan where an attempt has been made at integrating industrial and technological policies. However, such an integration requires an in-depth understanding of the domestic and international situation with regard to market and industrial structures, technological trends and capacity of technology absorption. In addition, suitable policy instruments need to be developed which may have to be modified over time in order to remain efficient. Above all, a competitive environment which does not allow individual companies to remain complacent and which poses a constant challenge to them, should be provided.

Concluding Remarks

To sum up, the following conclusions seem to emerge from the foregoing discussion :

First, the government has to play a crucial role in the upgrading of technology. It is necessary to augment the flow of resources to R&D by introducing fiscal and other incentives. However, before introducing new incentives, it is advisable to undertake a comprehensive study on the existing incentives and their impact in promoting R&D activity.

Second, at this stage of India's economic development, it has become imperative to integrate technology policy with industrial policy. Suitable institutional framework should be evolved in this regard. It is equally necessary to reform the present educational system so that adequately qualified people are available to man R&D projects.

Third, due emphasis has to be given to building up a comprehensive technology information system. For this purpose, specific needs of different types of end-users of technology information should first be identified and then a suitable system of consolidating the technology information from the micro level to the macro level should be evolved.

Fourth and the most important, the government has excessively directed and controlled the Indian economy. This has stifled the competitive element among individual companies. It is extremely necessary to pursue the policy of liberalisation so that companies are not scared to face competition. The business environment should provide both challenge and opportunity to individual enterprises. This would eventually make them more competitive both within and outside the country.

NOTES

1. Government of India, Ministry of Science and Technology, Department of Scientific and Industrial Research : *Promotion and Support to Indigenous Technology*, Delhi, February 1988.
2. Government of India, Department of Science and Technology : *Technology Policy and Statement*, New Delhi, January 1983.
3. Desai, Ashok V. : "Technological Performance in Indian Industry : The Influence of Market Structures and Policies" *in Technology Absorption in Indian Industry* edited by Ashok V. Desai, New Delhi, Wiley Eastern Limited, 1988, p.27.
4. Ibid., p.27.
5. Based on Seshagiri, N. : *Guidelines for the Formulation of National Industrial and Technological Information Policies* — Based on Indian Experience, UNIDO/IS-605, 27 January, 1986.
6. Based on Stoneman, Paul : *The Economic Analysis of Technology Policy*, Oxford, Clarendon Press, 1987, pp.36-39.
7. Rothwell, R. : "The Difficulties of National Innovation Policies" *in* S. Macdonald et al. (eds.), *The Trouble with Technology*, London, Francis Pinter, 1983.
8. Eragas, H. : "Does Technology Policy Matter," *in* P. Dasgupta and P. Stoneman (eds.), *Economic Policy and Technological Performance*, Cambridge, Cambridge University Press, 1987.
9. Based on Jon Sigurdson : *Integration of Industrial and Technology Policies in Japan : A Preliminary View*, UNIDO/IS., 633, 26 May, 1986.

8

RESEARCH AND DEVELOPMENT STATISTICS IN INDIA

Introduction

In Chapter 3, the official statistics on Research and Development were analysed in considerable detail, highlighting growth and pattern of R&D activity in India. In this chapter, major limitations of such statistics are identified. In addition, certain suggestions are made for their improvement. However, before commenting on R&D statistics, it seems worthwhile to briefly review their evolution.

Evolution of R&D Statistics

The first attempt to collect data on expenditure incurred on scientific research in India was made in 1958. The data related to the years 1955-56 and 1956-57 and were compiled from the demand for grants of the Central ministries, the State governments, the records of the UGC, etc. These data had a number of limitations and, as such, were not considered reliable. In the following year, data were collected through a specially designed questionnaire which was mailed to scientific institutions and universities. A similar attempt was made in 1961. Data collected through these questionnaires did not cover several institutions on account of lack of response on their part. During the period 1962-68, a number of meetings were held under the auspices of different agencies/bodies to devise methods and procedures for collection of data on S&T but with very limited success.

In 1971, the Department of Science and Technology was set up by the Government of India. Within this Department, a separate Science and Technology Statistics Division (STSD)has been entrusted with the responsibility of undertaking studies on S&T activities. The first comprehensive publication containing data on

R&D in the country was brought out for 1973-74. It was entitled "Research and Development Statistics, 1973-74". This publication is brought out at periodic intervals. The latest report relates to the year 1990-91.

A companion volume entitled "Research and Development in Industry" is also brought out from time to time, the latest one being for the year 1990-91. It may be noted that the coverage of these publications has expanded over the years.

The importance of R&D statistics for formulating and implementing science and technology policies cannot be over emphasized. A sound database will be extremely useful to the planners. Accordingly, a serious effort should be made to review the current R&D statistics in India, to point out their shortcomings and to suggest how such statistics can be improved.

It may be mentioned that this is perhaps the first occasion when R&D statistics compiled and analysed by the DST are being reviewed comprehensively. The purpose is not to find fault on trivial aspects but to improve their quality and coverage, and make them more accurate and more comparable. The chapter deals with DST's two publications "Research and Development Statistics" and "Research and Development in Industry". As the former publication is more comprehensive, our comments are mostly on the statistics contained in it.

A Critical Review of R&D Statistics

1. *Need for Brief Explanation of Concepts Used*

Research and Development Statistics are collected, tabulated, analysed and published by the DST once in every two years. The statistics are given for a number of years. It is necessary that certain concepts used in the publication are briefly and clearly explained for the benefit of the users.

A number of concepts/terms are used. To mention some of the more important ones : R&D activity, basic research, applied research, experimental development, R&D expenditure, R&D expenditure at constant prices, number of patents sealed, etc. A brief explanation of these concepts at the beginning of the publication would be very helpful to the users of such statistics. As the Annual Survey of Industries, another publication of the Government of India gives a brief explanation of each of the terms used in the annual survey, on the same lines, the Department of Science and Technology should give the explanation of the key terms used.

2. *Need for Balanced Coverage*

Since the publication of its first volume on R&D Statistics, the DST has expanded the scope of its publications: 1982-83,1984-85, 1986-87 and 1988-89, we find that the number of tables has increased.

R&D Statistics for the Year	No. of Tables given at the end
1982-83	16
1984-85	38
1986-87	34
1988-89	44
1990-91	41

Except in 1986-87 and 1990-91 when the number of tables has declined slightly, more and more tables are given by the DST. However, if we look more closely its publication, we find that a large number of tables are just based on S&T personnel. For example, the 1988-89 statistical publication contains as many as 18 tables on S&T personnel and related aspects. The 1990-91 publication contains 17 such tables. There must be some purpose in giving such tables. Simply because some of these statistics are readily available in UGC publications, they are given in the same form, does not seem to be appropriate. The DST should carefully go through these statistics and examine their suitability keeping in mind that the main focus is on R&D. There must be some balance between R&D tables and those on S&T personnel including enrolment and other aspects.

3. *Estimate of Non-Response*

The DST sends out its questionnaire on R&D to all units registered with it in respect of R&D activity. Since it is an official organisation, understandably a large number of units must be responding to the questionnaire. They must be returning the questionnaire, duly filled in, as per the instructions contained therein. Moreover, as many of these units fill in such a questionnaire once in every two years, they would not be experiencing any difficulty in this regard. However, some new units may find difficulty in supplying the requisite data.

They may not return the filled-in questionnaire. In addition, some other units may avoid sending the filled-in questionnaire. This results into non-response.

The DST publication mentions at some place, that an estimate of non-response has been made. No further details are given. In a publication of this type, it is desirable to have some more information on the extent of non-response. The DST should also explain the method used in estimating the R&D expenditure from units which have not responded.

4. *More Rational Approach for Projections*

Each R&D Statistics publication gives the data for the latest year on the basis of certain projections. The rates that are applied for projecting the figures for the latest year are : 15 per ent growth rate for central sector; 12 per cent growth rate for the state sector and 20 per cent growth for private sector. The same rates were applied in the preceding publication as well. Later on, in the subsequent publication the actual R&D expenditure data for that particular year are given.

The question is : how is this practice useful? This publication is expected to give the actual expenditure on R&D activity in the different sectors. Perhaps, the timing of collection and publication of these statistics may be so adjusted that the responding units are in a position to give their actual expenditure to the DST. This would avoid the need for making projections at arbitrary rates. The growth rates used appear to be arbitrary as they have remained unchanged over the past several years. Moreover, there is no explanation in support of the rates used for making projections.

In case the projections are unavoidable, then a more rational approach in choosing the growth rates is called for. For this purpose, it is necessary to examine carefully the data for the recent period, say for the past three years. In addition, factors that are likely to influence R&D activity should be considered while making projections.

5. *Use of GNP as Price Deflator*

Table 3 of the aforesaid publication gives R&D expenditure both at current and constant prices. The latter series is at the 1980-81 price. For converting R&D expenditure at current prices into 1980-81 (constant) price, the DST has used GNP price deflator as per Economic Survey 1991-92.

The question is : whether this GNP price deflator is appropriate? The nature of R&D expenditure is very different. It broadly comprises capital expenditure on equipment, plants and machinery and salaries of R&D personnel. Price changes in these two components would normally be different over a period of time. Perhaps the most suitable price deflator would be a composite index covering price changes in capital equipment and salary component. As such, a special series may have to be used for this purpose.

If, however, this is not undertaken as the amount of work involved may be too much, the wholesale price index for the machinery group may be used. This would perhaps be better than the GNP price deflator which is being used at present. In any case, this issue needs to be properly examined by statisticians and officials of the DST.

6. *Need for Expanding Coverage*

The DST collects detailed data on the number of employees as also the number of R&D personnel from each responding R&D unit. Some of these data are given in a number of tables contained in its publication Research and Development Statistics. However, it is advisable to give these data along with some other variables. For example, Table 11 gives data on (a) R&D expenditure and (b) R&D expenditure as percentage of sales turnover by major industry groups for the latest three years in respect of public sector industrial units. Table 12 gives similar data for private sector industrial units. It is advisable to expand the coverage of both these tables by providing data on (i) the number of employees and (ii) the number of R&D personnel. This additional information would enhance the utility of these tables. One would see from such statistics as to how the availability of a large number of R&D personnel is related to R&D expenditure in respect of different industry groups.

7. *R&D Expenditure by Private Sector Units*

Table 6 of the DST publication gives R&D expenditure by State governments. There is no table which provides R&D expenditure data in private sector industrial units in different states. It would be desirable to provide data on R&D expenditure by private sector units for the latest three years for different states on the lines of Table 6. Such data would enable the reader to have a comparative idea of R&D expenditure in private sector units/State governments in different states.

8. *Break-up of R&D Expenditure into Basic Research, Applied Research, etc.*

Table 8 of the DST publication gives the break-up of expenditure on science and technology under the following four heads : Basic research, Applied research, Experimental Development and Other Related S&T Activities. The first three components form the expenditure on R&D. These statistics are given for the latest three years separately in respect of Central Government and State Governments. Similar data for industrial units are not available. The scope of this table needs to be expanded so as to cover the industrial units both in the private and public sectors. Although private sector will normally spend far more on applied research, experimental development and other activities, provision of such statistics would enable the user to have a comparative idea of these activities in the private sector units.

9. *Data on R&D Personnel*

While the data on R&D expenditure are reasonably detailed both in respect of public and private sectors, corresponding data on R&D personnel are not given. It may be worthwhile to give a separate table for the past three years in which data are given for the following components : (a) R&D expenditure; (b) Persons engaged primarily in R&D activities; (c) Persons engaged in auxiliary activities; (d) Persons engaged in administrative activities; and (e) Total number of persons employed in R&D establishments. These data should be given separately for public sector and private sector industrial units. Such data over a period of time would be helpful in ascertaining the trend in the two series as also the extent of relationship between them.

10. *Break-Up of R&D Expenditure*

R&D Statistics relate to expenditure on R&D and other related aspects. The break-up of R&D expenditure is not given. However, in another publication on Research & Development in Industry, the DST does give the broad break-up of R&D expenditure under three heads namely, 'revenue', 'capital' and 'not classified'. It is desirable to show more classified data in this regard. For example, salaries of R&D personnel form a sizeable proportion of R&D expenditure both in the public and private sectors. There does not seem to be any difficulty in obtaining such data along with total R&D expenditure from industrial units. The DST may also give the foreign exchange component of R&D expenditure. In fact, the questionnaire which used to be sent out to R&D registered units earlier contained this item. But the questionnaire in the 1990-91 publication does not show this item. The DST may reconsider its inclusion and give the necessary information on foreign exchange component.

11. *Statistics on Patents*

Section-D of the questionnaire meant for industrial units seeks information on several items including (a) patents sealed, (b) products, (c) processes, (d) import substitutes developed, and (e) design prototypes developed. However, this information is not given in the publication itself. Since this information is regarded as an output of R&D activity, it may be worthwhile to give it in the form of a table. Such data over a period of time would be very useful for analysis particularly when one wants to know how far R&D activity has resulted into the sealing of patents, development of new products and new production processes, etc.

12. *R&D Units and Indigenous Technology*

One additional information which is worth seeking from R&D units is whether they are primarily engaged in the development of an indigenous technology or in the adaptation of an imported technology. A unit which is engaged in both types of R&D activity may be required to indicate the amount spent on these two types of R&D activity.

13. *Data on Cooperative R&D Expenditure*

Table 7 of the DST publication presents R&D expenditure by cooperative research associations for the latest three years. The data relate to 13 cooperative research associations such as Indian Jute

Industry's Research Association, Tea Research Association and Automotive Research Association of India. Except R&D expenditure, no other data are available in regard to cooperative research associations.

It seems desirable to extend the coverage of these statistics. A few suggestions are made in this connection. First, the break-up of R&D expenditure into basic research, applied research, experimental development and other activities may be given. Second, the number of member units in each of the associations listed may be given. Third, the number of R&D personnel employed in these associations may also be given. This would indicate broadly the extent of R&D activity taken up in research associations. These suggestions, if carried out, will increase the scope of R&D statistics pertaining to cooperative research associations. In this context, we should not forget that in a developing country like India where a large number of industrial units cannot afford to undertake R&D activity on their own, the cooperative form of R&D would be extremely useful to them. Hence it is desirable to provide some more data relating to cooperative form of R&D.

14. *R&D Expenditure by Industrial Units by States*

The R&D expenditure by State Governments is given in Table 6 of the DST publication. The corresponding statistics for industrial units for different states are not given. It is necessary that R&D expenditure incurred by industrial units is shown by states in a separate table. In fact, an overall table indicating R&D expenditure by (i) Central Government, (ii) State Government, (iii) industrial units, and (iv) the total R&D expenditure covering these components by states should be given. This would give an idea about the states in which R&D activity has assumed greater importance.

It may be still better if along with R&D expenditure by industrial units for different states the number of industrial units reporting this expenditure is also shown. Such data will be more useful in undertaking analysis by states. These can be given only in respect of R&D expenditure in industry. A separate table other than the one mentioned in the preceding paragraph may be given for this purpose.

15. *Contributions made for R&D Activity*

Question IV in Section-B of Questionnaire II of the DST publication meant for industrial units engaged in R&D relates to financial contributions made by these units to – (a) cooperative research associations; (b) departments or universities; and (c) other research institutions. The responding units are asked to furnish this information for the latest three years. Surprisingly, this information though obtained by the DST, is not given in its publication. There does not seem to be any particular reason for withholding it. The DST should provide it in a separate table.

In fact, the information sought in Question IV pertains to specific research associations, departments or universities, and other research institutions. The DST can compile a list of all such organisations who have received contributions from R&D units. This list along with the contributions for R&D for the latest three years may be shown in another table. Such data would clearly indicate those organisations which are generally patronised by R&D units. This may be on account of the fact that more effective R&D is done by such associations.

16. *Statistics on R&D Capital Expenditure*

Table 10 of the DST publication gives data on R&D expenditure by public/joint sector undertakings, for 1990-91. The data relate to both Central and State sector undertakings. Some of the figures contained in the table are very unusual on account of their high magnitude. To mention a few cases : (i) R&D expenditure as a percentage of sales turnover for the Maharashtra Electronics Corporation Ltd., Pune was 122.78, (ii) for the Webel Crystals Ltd. (West Bengal), R&D expenditure formed 118 per cent of sales turnover, (iii) for the Haryana State Electronics Development Corporation R&D expenditure formed 44.33 per cent of sales turnover. Similarly, there are a few other public/joint sector undertakings where R&D expenditure was proportionately much higher in terms of sales turnover. The data for most of the units show that R&D expenditure was not even one per cent of sales turnover.

How are such data useful? These data in a way are misleading. It may be that in a particular year huge capital expenditure on R&D activity has been incurred by a unit, which gives an abnormally high percentage in terms of sales turnover. As such these data do not seem to be comparable.

17. *Data on Exports by R&D Units*

The Government is giving considerable importance to exports. In order to promote Indian exports, several incentives are offered to different types of industries. The publication on "R&D in Industry" at present does not give any data on export. It seems desirable that some information on exports effected by R&D industrial units is given. Preferably, the data on the total value of sales effected and the value of goods exported for a particular year should be shown.

18. *Data on Capital Employed*

Another important aspect on which data are not available is capital employed. It is common knowledge that R&D activity is highly capital intensive. Generally, large units are engaged in R&D activity. As such, a statistical publication of this type should classify R&D industrial units into four or five categories on the basis of amount of capital employed. The DST should then give R&D expenditure incurred separately for each of these categories.

19. *Discrepancies in R&D Expenditure Statistics*

Table 18 of this publication presents data on R&D expenditure by industry groups for small scale sector industries. These data pertain to three years – 1986-87, 1987-88 and 1988-89. However, it is not mentioned as to which definition of small scale industries has been used. Since the definition of small scale industrial units has changed from time to time, the definition used for the purpose of this table should be specified. These comments are also applicable to Table 21 which gives statistics on R&D expenditure by states.

There are certain discrepancies in R&D statistics as will be evident from Table 8.1. This table presents data for 1988-89 for three selected groups of industries published in the two publications. These data relate to small scale industries. It is intriguing to find that while the number of units in electricals and electronics equipment was larger in publication B, the expenditure on R&D was less as compared to the corresponding figure shown in Publication-A. Figures for the other two groups too show certain discrepancies as both sets of figures cannot be correct. If a comparison of statistics for 1988-89 contained in the two publications is made on an extensive scale, one may come across several discrepancies between them.

TABLE 8.1: Discrepancies in R&D Expenditure Statistics (1988-89)

Group	No. of Units	R&D Expenditure (Rs. lakhs)
Electricals & Electronics Equipment		
Publication-A	55	636.19
Publication-B	66	587.71
Industrial Machinery		
Publication-A	17	312.31
Publication-B	16	158.29
Chemicals		
Publication-A	46	220.50
Publication-B	46	329.62

Publication-A Research and Development in Industry 1988-89
Publication-B Research and Development in Industry 1990-91.

Summing Up

As mentioned in the introduction to this chapter, the purpose of critically reviewing the existing statistics is to offer suggestions for their improvement.

Since R&D statistics are vitally important for planning purposes, it is suggested that one or two experts from the Central Statistical Organisation (CSO) be involved in deciding the scope and process of collecting R&D statistics. It is not known whether the DST has the expert advice of the CSO at present. It would be worthwhile if the DST sets up an expert committee on R&D statistics for examining how best such statistics can be improved. A periodical review of such statistics say, once in every three or five years, may be desirable.

Finally, it should be emphasized that statistics are not an end in themselves but only a means to an end. A number of individuals, industrial enterprises apart from government departments are the end-users of official statistics. When statistics are available within the government, non-government users find it very difficult to have access to such statistics. It is desirable to plan for opening out statistical system to interested persons and enterprises outside the government. For example, if an interested individual wants to have detailed data on R&D for individual companies for his research work, the DST should ensure that he has an access to these statistics.

It is hoped that limitations of R&D statistics as also suggestions made for their improvement as given in this chapter would receive the attention of the DST.

9

CONCLUSIONS AND SUGGESTIONS

This chapter presents the conclusions reached in the study. In addition, some suggestions are made to promote R&D activity in India.

At this juncture, when the business environment in India is changing fast as a consequence of shift in the Government's industrial policy, it will be disastrous to remain indifferent to R&D activity. Promotion of exports, for example, is the crying need of the country in view of its precarious foreign exchange position. This can be achieved by improving the quality of existing products, introduction of new products, adoption of more economical processes of production, etc. through meaningful and well-coordinated R&D undertaken on a reasonably large scale.

Seen in this context of changing business environment in India, the findings of this study assume considerable importance. It is hoped that those concerned with the promotion of R&D both within and outside the government will give due consideration to these findings.

1. There appears to be close positive relationship between technological change and economic performance. A number of studies show that there is high rate of return to investment in R&D. As such, it is advisable to transfer the resources to R&D where returns are relatively high. Further, social rates of returns are bound to be higher than the private rates of return to R&D.
2. While the trend in R&D expenditure in India shows an impressive rise over the years, this impressive growth fades away if it is related to gross national product. India has just reached mere one per cent of its GNP devoted to R&D. This is a meagre proportion. A comparison with other countries shows that India is one of those countries which spend an extremely low proportion of their national income for R&D activity.

3. A large proportion of R&D expenditure is incurred by the Government sector. This means that industrial units in the private sector are indifferent towards R&D. R&D intensity which shows R&D expenditure as a percentage of sales has always remained very low. It is revealing that not even 70 paise are spent on R&D out of every Rs. 100 of sales effected by industrial enterprises.
4. An account of R&D activity in selected enterprises shows that there are divergent approaches used by them. This is understandable on account of a variety of factors such as structure of the industry, technology used in the industry, government policy, the extent of professionalisation and the financial position of the enterprise. At the same time one finds that successful enterprises in R&D have laid emphasis on certain aspects which happen to be common. These are : judicious selection of both R&D projects and R&D personnel, sufficient freedom to R&D personnel and existence of an effective communication system amongst all categories of employees.
5. As management has to play a vital role in strengthening R&D activity, it is suggested that suitable training programmes for R&D managers in industry be organised so as to have effective utilization of expenditure on R&D and to avoid wastage of resources which would otherwise occur. It is also suggested that a central organisation specifically for this purpose should be set up. Experts from industry, university and other institutions should be drawn for imparting training to R&D personnel.
6. There are instances which show that several incentives offered for undertaking R&D activity are being misused. This needs to be checked. The government should come out with new incentives. It is also desirable to have periodical reviews to ascertain the impact of different incentives on the growth of R&D activity.
7. It is necessary to undertake detailed review of science and engineering education in India. There is an imperative need to restructure in particular post-graduate science and engineering education so that such education can be more useful to the present state of the Indian economy.
8. Education, Research and Extension are the three spheres of activity for advanced educational institutions such as IITs and

universities. Of these, extension activity is the weakest link. The concept of extension in respect of engineering colleges and IITs is to integrate engineering sciences with industry, technology development and specialised production. This integration can be brought about if there is sufficient awareness among the Faculty of the social needs of the environment in which engineering institutions are working. At present there seems to be a general indifference for such extension activities. IITs should encourage their Faculty to take up projects which have social relevance such as development of alternative sources of energy. Such extension activities should be taken up in a much larger way than at present.

9. Some of the recommendations made by the IITs Review Committee in 1986 have not been implemented as yet. Since huge resources are channelised to IITs, the Government should ensure that (a) IITs restructure and revise their courses of study and (b) large scale migration of IIT graduates to foreign countries is reduced.
10. One of the weakest areas in R&D is the lack of institutional collaboration. The interaction between industry on the one hand and institutions such as universities, IITs and national laboratories on the other is extremely inadequate. A concerted effort should be made by the Government to bring about an effective association among these institutions to promote R&D. Further, it would be desirable to set up a consortium of companies, national laboratories, IITs and universities to undertake jointly R&D as is the practice in the Western countries.
11. Since R&D activity is highly capital intensive, small enterprises cannot be expected to undertake it on their own. While some financial incentives may be offered to encourage such enterprises to undertake R&D, a major thrust in the coming years should be to promote cooperative R&D. The industry associations should take initiative and in consultation with member-firms take up R&D projects of common interest.
12. A major factor responsible for poor utilization of research done in national laboratories is that the projects are selected regardless of their market potential. Marketing factor has generally been overlooked by R&D scientists. There should

be growing realisation to relate R&D activity with marketing.

13. The NRDC should reinforce its efforts in disseminating the results of R&D to industry. It should be further strengthened both in terms of financial and human resources so that it can play a more effective role than hitherto. It is desirable to reorganise it so that it functions efficiently and not like a government department. Further, it should set up new plants based on R&D done in national laboratories and sell them to entrepreneurs to minimise their risk.

14. Since R&D activity involves considerable uncertainty regarding the outcome, there is an inherent risk in it. There are various types of uncertainties such as attitude of labour to innovation, reaction of competitors and policies of the Government. All these uncertainties can be clubbed under 'human uncertainties'. In addition, there are physical uncertainties such as an apprehension that some snags may be found in the laboratory model or a pilot plant when used for the first time for commercial production. Also, there may be fear that the new product may not retain the properties which it has in the laboratory model. In view of these uncertainties, only a few enterprises are willing to take such a risk. Most of the enterprises are reluctant to do so. However, this hesitation and unwillingness on their part can be overcome to a certain extent if the Government or some other suitable organisation such as the National Research and Development Corporation introduces a scheme of insurance to compensate industrial enterprises for the losses that they might incur in R&D

    Another way to overcome hesitancy of industrial firms in regard to R&D activity is to see that the NRDC starts pilot plants as has been mentioned in (13) above. After a successful experimentation, the plant may be sold out to entrepreneurs who will then be willing to invest in it.

15. The Department of Science and Technology should make an earnest effort to improve R&D statistics. The coverage of its publication on R&D statistics should be enlarged and statistics on many related aspects, which are not covered at present, should be collected. The DST should also remove the major limitations of the present statistics.

    As a first step towards the improvement of R&D statistics, it is suggested that the DST should set up an expert committee comprising members from its own department, Central

Statistical Organisation, Indian Statistical Institute, National Institute of Science, Technology and Development Studies and NCAER so that all aspects in the compilation of R&D statistics can be properly looked into.The recommendations of such a committee will help improve Indian R&D statistics to a large extent. Apart from this, it is desirable that R&D statistics be reviewed periodically so that these can be improved from time to time.

APPENDICES

APPENDIX-I

UGC Research Project on Research and Development in Indian Industry

QUESTIONNAIRE

Opinion Survey of R&D Managers

(1) Name of the Company :
(2) Address :
(3) Name of the Manager :
(4) Age :
(5) Pay Scale :
(6) Is your organisation registered with S&T Department?
'Yes' _______ 'No' _______
(7) If 'yes', do you get any concession or facilities from them?
'Yes' _______ 'No' _______
(8) If yes, please specify the types of concessions or facilities.

(9) What post are your holding at present?

a) In-charge of a project
b) A Manager
c) A Section Leader
d) A Division Leader
e) Assistant Director
f) Director
g) Research Director

(10) What percentage of your weekly working time is spent on the following activities?

Activities	*Time (Hours)*
a) Research	________%
b) Administration	________%
c) Consultation and discussion with colleagues	________%
d) Library Research	________%
e) Discussion with similar officers	________%
f) Discussion with junior officers	________%
g) Any other activity (Please specify)	________%

(11) Would you prefer to spend more or less time on technical duties as opposed to administration/non-technical duties?

a) More ________
b) About the same ________
c) Less ________

(12) Which of the following types of training would help you to do your job better?

a) Technical training ________
b) Management training ________
c) Both Technical and Management training ________
d) Neither management nor technical ________

(13) How long have you been working in this organisation?

(14) Have you specialised in one or more areas?

Yes ________ No ________

(15) If yes, please specify area/s of specialisation.

(16) To what extent you are able to use your specialised knowledge in R&D activity?

a) Considerable
b) Moderate

c) Extremely inadequate

(17) Which of the following factors are considered by you, while selecting R&D Project? Please give priority.

a) The researcher's interest
b) Practicability
c) The urgency of the problem
d) Expected outcome
e) Availability of resources

(18) Below are given three types of research, please indicate broadly their relative shares in your total (100%) R&D activity.

a) Basic Research ______________________ %
b) Applied Research ______________________ %
c) Development Research ______________________ %

(19) If you are an applied scientist, please write the number of industrial units, institutes, laboratories and university departments, that you have recently visited.

Numbers
a) ______________________ Industrial units
b) ______________________ Institutes
c) ______________________ Laboratories
d) ______________________ University departments

(20) Which of the following objectives are applicable to your R&D activity?

a) To improve profitability
b) To improve the quality of product
c) To improve the competitiveness of your unit
d) To utilise the technical skill already available
e) To increase exports
f) To reduce dependence on imports
g) To overcome obsolescence
h) Any other (Please specify)

(21) Do you involve your staff while deciding on a research project?

Yes _______ No _______

(22) Can you briefly describe the procedure for selecting a research project?

(23) Is there any relationship between the present R&D project and the earlier one?

Yes _______ No _______

(24) How do you formulate programmes for the implementation of the project?

(25) Is there any mechanism for monitoring the progress in respect of selected R&D project?

Yes _______ No _______

(26) If yes, please give the procedure of monitoring.

(27) While selecting research staff, how do you make recruitment?

a) From the open market
b) Within the organisation

(28) While selecting a researcher, which of the following consideration do you generally keep in mind?

a) Technical competence
b) Length of experience
c) Training in foreign countries
d) Standing within your organisation

(29) What quality of S&T personnel is found in your organisation?

a) Extremely good
b) Good

c) Moderately good
d) Moderately poor
e) Poor
f) Extremely poor

(30) In your R&D project do you feel handicapped on account of shortages of qualified manpower?
Yes _______ No _______

(31) If yes, what are the reasons?

(32) Please give the following information about foreign trained manpower's perception of work environment in India and abroad

Manpower's Perception of work	Work Environment in India		
	Better than abroad	Same as abroad	Worse than abroad
a) Independence of work			
b) General atmosphere			
c) Equipments and Supplies			
d) Job conditions			
e) Salary			
f) Supervisor's ability			

(33) How good R&D activities are being managed?

a) Very well managed
b) Satisfactorily managed
c) Poorly managed
d) Very poorly managed

(34) Is there sufficient opportunity to follow up interesting research findings in the course of your work?

a) Usually
b) Occasionally
c) Seldom

(35) Do you have the practice of holding department meetings periodically?

Yes ______ No ______

(36) If yes, how effective are these meetings for promoting R&D?

a) Extremely effective
b) Fairly effective
c) Satisfactory
d) Somewhat effective
e) Extremely in-effective

(37) What types of difficulties have been faced while undertaking R&D?

a) Shortages of particular skills
b) Financial Constraint
c) Shortage of raw-material
d) Government regulations
e) Indifferent attitude of management
f) Any other (Please specify)

(38) Have you ever dropped a R&D project without completing it?

Yes ______ No ______

(39) If yes, in which year?

Name of the project
Reasons

(40) Which of the following incentive/s is/are generally given to researcher for encouraging them?

a) Security of job
b) Special reward for meritorious R&D work
c) Provision of bonus
d) Higher salary
e) Profit sharing
f) Better working condition

g) Sufficient freedom to work
h) Freedom to publish research papers
i) Opportunity for training in foreign countries

(41) How do you overcome slow progress of the project or inefficiency of R&D work?

a) By giving him little warning to improve the performance
b) By providing him extra/additional training
c) By changing the nature of work
d) By asking him to leave
e) By demoting
f) By dismissal

(42) Which of the following condition/s could induce you to leave your present company?

a) Higher salary ____________________
b) Improved working conditions ____________________
c) Better research facilities ____________________
d) Increased responsibility ____________________
e) Any other (Please specify) ____________________

(43) Would you like to make any other observation on R&D with respect to your organisation?

APPENDIX II

INCENTIVES AVAILABLE TO R&D UNITS

The Government of India has been offering certain incentives to industrial units for promoting R&D activity. These incentives have changed from time to time. The incentives listed below are based on the latest official document:*

1. Import Facilities

All the recognised in-house R&D units as well as institutions can import their full requirements of raw materials, technical and professional equipment, components, spares or other items under the Open General Licence (OGL). Subject to certain conditions, they can also import proto-types, samples and pilot items. This facility is not available for the import of consumer goods and office machines.

2. Custom Duty Exemption

The scientific and industrial research organisations (SIROs) recognised by the DSIR are entitled for custom duty exemption for the import of items relating to capital equipment, spares and raw materials required for their R&D projects. This exemption is not available to in-house R&D units.

3. Income-tax Relief

Under Section 35(1)(i) of the Income-tax Act, the revenue expenditure incurred on scientific research by the in-house R&D units relating to its business is allowed as full deduction. Capital expenditure too can be fully deducted from the income of the year in which it is incurred under Section 35(2) of the Income-tax Act. Further, any contributions made to SIROs approved by DSIR and notified under Section 35(1)(ii)/(ii) of the Income Tax Act are also exempted from income-tax.

---

* Based on Department of Scientific and Industrial Research: *Research and Development by Industry: An Overview*, 1992.

4. Accelerated Depreciation Allowance

In order to encourage the use of indigenous technology, depreciation allowance at a higher rate of 40 per cent is available in respect of plant and machinery installed for the production of goods based on indigenous technology.

5. Exemption from Drugs (Price Control) Order, 1987

The production of bulk drugs from basic stage by process developed through indigenous R&D is eligible for exemption from price control for a period up to five years. This exemption is also applicable to the processes developed by national laboratories and acquired and used by the manufacturing company.

6. International R&D Collaborations

A scheme for promoting international R&D collaborations at the enterprise/institution level has been introduced by the Government under which the DSIR approves and issues clearance to proposals involving R&D collaborations between Indian companies/ institutions and those in foreign countries. In addition, financial assistance to a limited extent can be provided to the concerned company/institution.

7. Financial Support for R&D Programmes

R&D units and SIROs are provided financial support in priority areas for commercialisation of processes developed through in-house R&D/SIRO system up to bench scale/pilot scale. Financial support is also available for technology absorption programmes.

8. National Awards for R&D Efforts

There is a scheme of the DSIR, effective from 1988, for giving national awards to recognised R&D units for their outstanding R&D activity.

9. Indirect Benefits

In addition to the incentives and support schemes mentioned above,

R&D units and SIROs have some indirect benefits. They enjoy a good deal of credibility for obtaining financial assistance for R&D from financial institutions. They are also able to attract competent technical personnel for R&D projects. Further, they get recognition from universities as approved centres for conducting research for the award of higher degrees.

BIBLIOGRAPHY

Alam, Ghayur and John Langrish : "Government Research and its Utilisation by Industry : The Case of Industrial Civil Research in India", *Research Policy*, Vol. 13, No. 1. , February 1984, pp. 55-61.

Allio, Robert J. and Desmond Sheeham : "Allocating R&D Resources Effectively", *Research Management*, Vol. 27 (4), 1984, pp. 14-20.

Anderson, A. M. : *Science and Technology in Japan*, London, Longman Group Ltd. , 1984.

Bergen, S. A. and R. Miyajima : "Productivity and the R&D/Production Interface in Japan", *R&D Management*, Vol. 16, No. 1, January 1988, pp. 15-24.

Beri, G. C. : "Research and Development Activity in India", *Productivity*, Vol. XXI, No. 2, July-Sept, 1980, pp. 153-163.

——— : "Management of Research and Development", *Productivity*, Vol. XXIV, No. 2, 1983, pp. 179-184.

Bidkar, Ira R. : *Sources of Innovation : An Economic Analysis*, Bombay, Himalaya Publishing House, 1991.

Bluementhal, T. : "A Note on the Relationship between Domestic Research and Development and Imported Technology", *Economic Development and Cultural Change*, Vol. 27, No. 2.

Bollinger, Lynn, Katherine Hope and James M. Utterback : "A Review of Literature and Hypotheses on New Technology – Based Firms", *Research Policy*, Vol. 12, No. 1, February 1983, pp. 15-36.

Bonnet, Didier C. L. : "Nature of the R&D/Marketing Cooperation in the Design of Technologically Advanced New Industrial Products", *R&D Management*, Vol. 16, No. 2, April 1986, pp. 117-126.

Bozeman, Barry and Albert N. Link : "Tax Incentives for R&D : A Critical Evaluation", *Research Policy*, Vol. 13, No. 1, February 1984, pp. 21-31.

Brown and Svenson : "Measuring R&D Productivity", *Research and Technology Management*, July-August, 1988.

Burns, T. and G. M. Stalker : *The Management of Innovation*, London, Tavistock Publications, 1965.

Carter, Charles (ed.) : *Industrial Policy and Innovation,* Hants (U. K.), Gower Publishing Co. Ltd. , 1981.

Chaudhuri, Shekhar : "Technology Development for Commercial Industry", *Productivity*, Vol. XXV, No. 1, 1984, pp. 27-34.

—— : "Technology Innovation in a Research Laboratory in India : A Case Study", *Research Policy*, Vol. 15, 1986, pp. 89-103.

Chowdhury, P. N. : *Economics of Research and Development*, New Delhi, People's Publishing House, 1973.

Cohen, W. M. and D. A. Levinthal : "Innovation and Learning : The Two Faces of R&D", *Economic Journal*, Vol. 99, No. 397, Sept. 1989, pp. 569-596.

Collier, Donald W. *et al.* : "How Effective is Technological Innovation?", *Research Management*, Vol. 27, No. 5, 1984, pp. 11-16.

Confederation of Engineering Industry : Papers presented at the Fourth National Conference on In-House R&D in Industry, 22-23 November, 1990, New Delhi (mimeographed).

Dasgupta, P. & J. Stiglitz : " Industrial Structure and the Nature of Innovative Activity", *Economic Journal*, Vol. 90, No. 358, 1980, pp. 226-293.

Dasgupta, P. and P. Stoneman (eds.) : *Economic Policy and Technological Performance*, Cambridge, Cambridge University Press, 1987.

Davies, S. : *The Diffusion of Process Innovations*, Cambridge, Cambridge University Press, 1979.

Dean, B. V. and J. L. Goldhar (eds.) : *Management of Research and Innovation*, TIMS Studies in the Management Sciences, North-Holland Publishing Company, 1980.

Desai, Ashok V. : "Research and Development in India", *Margin*, January 1975.

—— : "The Origin and Direction of Industrial R&D in India", *Research Policy*, Vol. 9, 1980, p. 74.

——: "India's Technological Capability : An Analysis of its Achievements and Limits", *Research Policy*, Vol. 13, No. 5, Oct. 1984, pp. 303-310.

—— : "Market Structure and Technology : Their Interdependence in Indian Industry", *Research Policy*, Vol. 14, No. 3, June 1985, pp. 161-170.

Desai, Ashok V. : (ed.) : *Technology Absorption in Indian Industry*, New Delhi, Wiley Eastern Ltd. , 1988.

Economic and Scientific Research Foundation : *Technology Policy*, New Delhi, E. S. R. F. ,1983.

Evenson, R. E. and G. Rains (eds.) : *Science and Technology : Lessons for Development Policy*, Boulder, Colo. , Westview, 1990.

Firestone, O. J. : *Economic Implications of Patents*, University of Ottawa Press, 1971.

Francis, Arthur : *New Technology at Work*, Oxford, Oxford University Press.

Freeman, C. : *The Economics of Industrial Innovation*, London, Frances Pinter,1982 (2nd edition).

Geoffrey, Wyatt : *The Economics of Innovation*, Brighton, Wheatsheaf Books, 1986.

Goldsmith, Maurice (ed.) : *Technological Innovation and the Economy*, London, Wiley-Inter Science (A Division of John Wiley & Sons Ltd.), 1970.

Government of India, Ministry of Education and Culture (Department of Education) : *Report of the IIT Review Committee*, New Delhi, 1986.

Grilches, Z. (ed.) : *R&D : Patents and Productivity*, Chicago, University of Chicago Press, 1984.

Hall, P. (ed.) : *Technology, Innovation and Economic Policy*, Oxford, Philip Allan, 1986.

Holloman, J. Herbert : "Government and the Innovation Process", *Technology Review*, Vol. 81 (6), May 1979, pp. 30-41.

Israel, Dror and Rubenstein Albert H. : "Top Management Roles in R&D Projects", *R&D Management*, Vol. 14, No. 1, 1984, pp. 37-46.

Joshi, S. S. , J. V. Rajan and S. K. Subramanian : "The Indian Patent System and Indigenous R&D", *Research Policy*, Vol. 3, 1974.

Kamien, M. and Schwartz, N. : *Market Structure and Innovation*, Cambridge, Cambridge University Press, 1982.

Katrak, H. : "Imported Technology, Enterprise Size and R&D in a Newly Industrialising Country : The Indian Experience", *Oxford Bulletin of Economics and Statistics*, Vol. 47, No. 3, 1985.

—— : "Imported Technologies and R&D in a Newly Industrialising Country : The Experience of Indian Enterprises, *Journal of Development Economics*, 32, 1989.

Kay, N. M. : *The Innovating Firm*, London, Macmillan, 1979.

Kumar, Muneesh : *International Transfer of Technology to India*, New Delhi, Anmol Publications,1988.

Kumar, N. "Technology Imports and Local Research and Development in Indian Manufacturing", *The Developing Economics*, Vol. XXV, No. 3, September 1987.

Krishaiah, V. S. R. and Prithpal Singh : "Measuring Effectiveness of R&D Groups", *Productivity*, Vol. 29, No. 1, April-June 1988, pp. 73-80.

Layton, Christopher *et al.* : *Ten Innovations*, London, George Allen & Unwin Ltd. , 1972.

Link, Albert N. : *Research and Development Activity in U. S. Manufacturing*, New York, Praeger, 1981.

Lyons, B. : "International Technology Policy" *in* P. Dasgupta and P. Stoneman (eds.), *Economic Policy and Technological Performance*, Cambridge, Cambridge University Press, 1987.

Macdonald, J. M. : "Research and Development and the Directions of Diversification", *Review of Economics and Statistics*, Vol. 67, Nov. 1985, pp. 583-590.

Macdonald *et al.* (eds.) : *The Trouble with Technology*, London, Frances Pinter, 1983.

Mansfield, E. : "The R&D Tax Credit and other Technology Policy Issues", *American Economic Review*, Vol. 76, No. 2, 1986, pp. 190-194.

—— *et al*: "Social and Private Rates of Return from Industrial Innovations", *Quarterly Journal of Economics*, Vol. 91, No. 2, May 1977, pp. 221-240.

—— : *Technology Transfer, Productivity and Economic Policy*, New York, W. W. Norton, 1982.

McLeod, Tom : *The Management of Research, Development and Design Industry*, Hants (England), Gower Technical Press, 1988 (2nd edition).

Moravesik, Michael J. : "The Role of Science and Technology Transfer", *Research Policy*, Vol. 12, No. 3, October 1983, pp. 287-296.

More, Roger A. : "Patterns of Market Research Timing for New Industrial Products", *R&D Management*, Vol. 15, No. 4, 1985, pp. 271-282.

Mortan, J. A. : *Organising for Innovation*, New York, McGraw-Hill, 1971.

Moss, Thomas H. : *Innovation Management in Developing Countries*, Vienna, UNIDO, October 1985 (UNIDO/IS. 566) (mimeographed).

Myers, S. and D. G. Marquis : *Successful Industrial Innovation*, Washington, National Science Foundation, 1969.

National Science Foundation : *National Patterns of Science and Technology Resources*, Washington, N. S. F. , 1984.

Nelson, R. (ed.) : *The Rate and Direction of Inventive Activity*, Princeton, N. J. , Princeton University Press, 1982.

—— : *Government and Technical Progress*, New York, Pergamon Press, 1982.

—— : *High Technology Policies : A Five Nation Comparison*, Washington, American Enterprise Institute for Public Policy Research, 1984.

Norris, K. and J. Vaizey : *The Economics of Research and Technology*, London, George Allen & Unwin, 1973.

Nystrom, H. : *Creativity and Innovation*, Chichester, John Wiley & Sons, 1979.

Odagiri, Hiroyuki and Hitoshi Iwata, : "The Impact of R&D on Productivity Increase in Japanese Manufacturing Companies", *Research Policy*, Vol. 15, No. 1, Feb. 1986, pp. 13-19.

O.E.C.D. : *Policies for the Stimulation of Industrial Innovation*, Country Reports, Vol. 2-1, Paris, 1978.

——: *Technical Change and Economic Policy*, Paris, 1980.

—— : *The Measurement of Scientific and Technical Activities : Proposed Standard Practice for Surveys of Research and Experimental Development* (Frascati Manual), Paris, 1981.

—— : *Science and Technology Indicators*, Basic Statistical Series, Paris, 1983.

—— : *Industry and University : New Forms of Cooperation and Communication*, Paris, 1984.

——: *Science and Technology Policy Outlook*, Paris, 1985.

—— : *Science and Technology Indicators 2 : R&D, Invention and Competitiveness*, Paris, 1986.

—— : Papers presented at the International Seminar on Science, Technology, and Economic Growth, June 5-8, 1989.

Palda, Kristian S. : "Technological Intensity : Concept and Measurement", *Research Policy*, Vol. 15, No. 4, August 1986, pp. 187-198.

Pangasa, Rakesh : "Objectivity in Industrial Research : Organizational Effectiveness and Efficiency", *Productivity*, Vol. 23, No. 2, July-Sept. 1982, pp. 171-189.

Pappas, Richard A. and Donald S. Remer : "Measuring R&D Productivity", *Research Management*, Vol. XXVIII, No. 3, May-June 1985.

Parker, Charles : *Innovate through Technology*, London, The British Institute of Management, 1989.

Parker, J. E. S. : *The Economics of Innovation*, London, Longman, 1978 (2nd edition).

Parker, R. C. : *The Management of Innovation*, Chicester, John Wiley & Sons, 1982.

—— : *Going for Growth*, Chicester, John Wiley & Sons, 1985.

Pavitt, Keith : "R&D, Patenting and Innovative Activities : A Statistical Exploration", *Research Policy*, Vol. 11, No. 1, February 1982, pp. 33-51.

Pavitt, K. and S. Wald : *The Conditions for Success in Technological Innovation*, Paris, O. E. C. D. , 1971.

Piatier, A. : *Barriers to Innovation*, London, Frances Pinter, 1984.

Pickett, J. and R. Robson : *Manual on the Choice of Industrial Technique in Developing Countries*, Paris, O. E. C. D. , 1986.

Peters, T. J. & R. H. Waterman : *In Search of Excellence : Lessons from America's Best-Run Companies*, New York, Harper & Row, 1982.

Prasad, A. J. : *Technology Policy for Industry*, Bombay, Allied Publishers Pvt. Ltd. , 1979.

Radosevich, R. and Robles F. : "Improving Matrix Relationships in R&D Organisations – Marketing Support Services", *R&D Management*, Vol. 14, No. 4, 1984, pp. 229-232.

Roberts, E. B. : *The Dynamics of Research and Development*, New York, Harper & Row, Publishers, 1964.

—— (ed.) : *Generating TechnologicaL Innovation*, New York and Oxford, Oxford University Press, 1987.

Rogers, E. M. : *The Diffusion of Innovations*, New York, Free Press, 1983.

Roman, D. D. and J. F. Puett : *International Business and Technological Innovation*, New York, Elsevier, 1982.

Rosenberg, N. : "Science, Invention and Economic Growth", *Economic Journal*, Vol. 84, 1974, pp. 90-108.

—— : *Perspectives on Technology*, Cambridge, Cambridge University Press, 1976.

Rosenberg, N. : *Inside the Black Box : Technology and Economics, Cambridge*, Cambridge University Press, 1982.

—— : and C. Frischtak (eds.) : *International Technology Transfer : Concepts, Measures and Comparisons*, New York, Praeger, 1985.

Sankar, T. L. , R. K. Mishra, A. S. Sastry and S. Ravishankar : *Management of Research and Development in Public Sector*, Bombay, Himalaya Publishing House, 1986.

Scherer, F. M. : *Innovation and Growth*, Cambridge, Mass. , M. I. T. Press, 1984.

Seshagiri, N. : *Guidelines for the Formulation of National Industrial and Technological Information Policies – Based on Indian Experience*, Vienna, UNIDO, January 1986 (UNIDO/IS. 605) (mimeographed).

Singh, Baldev : "Research and Development in Industry", *Economic and Political Weekly*, 22 (34), 22 August, 1987, pp. 1431-1434.

Smith, W. Novis, E. Gerald Meyer and Alan R. Hirsig (eds.) : *Industrial R&D Management – The Modern Issues*, New York, Marcel Dekrer, Inc. , 1982.

Spacy, J. (for UNESCO) : *Science for Development*, Paris,1971.

Stoneman, P. : *The Economic Analysis of Technological Change*, Oxford, Oxford University Press, 1983.

—— : *The Economic Analysis of Technology Policy*, Oxford, Clarendon Press, 1987.

Srinivasan, M. : *Management of Science and Technology : Problems and Prospects*, New Delhi, Affiliated East-West Press Pvt. Ltd. , 1989.

Subrahmanian, K. K. : "Technological Capability under Economic Liberalism - Experience of Indian Industry in Eighties", *Economic and Political Weekly*, August 31, 1991, pp. M-87-M-92.

Sveikanskas, L. : "The Contribution of R&D to Productivity Growth", *Monthly Labour Review*, Vol. 109, March 1986, pp. 16-20.

Taylor, C. T and Z. A. Silberston : *The Economic Impact of the Patent System*, Cambridge, Cambridge University Press,1973.

Teece, David J. : "Profiting from Technological Innovation : Implications for Integration, Collaboration, Licensing and Public Policy", *Research Policy*, Vol. 15, No. 6, Dec. 1986, pp. 285-305.

Tisdell, C. A. : *Science and Technology Policy – Priorities of Governments*, London, Chapman and Hall, 1981.

Tolley, G. S. et al. (eds.) : *The Economics of R&D Policy*, New York, Praeger, 1985.

UNESCO : *The Effectiveness of Research Groups in Six Countries*, Cambridge, Cambridge University Press & UNESCO, Paris, 1979.

UNIDO : *UNIDO Programme on Technological Advances*, Vienna, UNIDO, August 1987 (IPCT, 39 (SPEC) (mimeographed).

UNIDO : India : *New Dimensions of Industrial Growth*, Oxford, Basil Blackwell, 1990 (Industrial Development Review Series of UNIDO).

Verschuur, J. J. : *Technologies and Markets*, Stevenage, Peter Peregrinus Ltd. , 1984.

Williams, Bruce : "The Direct and Indirect Role of Higher Education in Industrial Innovation : What should we Expect?", *Minerva*, Vol. XXIV, Nos. 2-3, Summer-Autumn, 1986, pp. 145-171.

Wright, B. D. : "The Economics of Invention Incentives : Patents, Prizes and Research Contracts ", *American Economic Review*, Vol. c 73, No. 4, 1983, pp. 691-707.

INDEX